P9-CQA-175

# Uncle John's Bathroom Reader®

# ROBOTICA

**BATHROOM READERS' PRESS**

ASHLAND, OREGON

"I am superior, sir, in many ways. But I would gladly give it up to be human."

—**Data, *Star Trek: The Next Generation***

"Man is a robot with defects."

—**Emile Cioran, *The Trouble with Being Born***

UNCLE JOHN'S BATHROOM READER®

# ROBOTICA



For information, write: The Bathroom Readers' Institute,
P.O. Box 1117, Ashland, OR 97520
www.bathroomreader.com

Cover and interior design by Andy Taray – Ohioboy.com

ISBN-10: 1-62686-176-5 – ISBN-13: 978-1-62686-176-3

Library of Congress Cataloging-in-Publication Data

Uncle John's bathroom reader robotica.

pages cm

ISBN 978-1-62686-176-3 (pbk.)

1. Robots--Miscellanea. 2. Robotics--Miscellanea. 3. American wit and humor. I. Bathroom Readers' Institute (Ashland, Or.) II. Title: Bathroom reader robotica.

TJ211. U53 2014

629.8'92--dc23

2013048502

Printed in the United States of America
First Printing: September 2014
1 2 3 4 5 18 17 16 15 14

# THANK YOU!

*The Bathroom Readers' Institute sincerely thanks the people whose advice and assistance made this book possible.*

Gordon Javna

Brian Boone

Andy Taray

Kevin Shellhouse

Trina Janssen

Joan Kyzer

Brandon Hartley

Pablo Goldstein

Scott Eckert

Megan Todd

Ben Godar

Matt Springer

Michael Conover

Erica Richman

Jay Newman

Eric Dodson

Kim Griswell

Lindsay Gillingham Taylor

Aaron Guzman

David Hoye

Blake Mitchum

Jennifer, Ginger, and Mana

PeetR NOR-TON

Lilian Nordland

Bender Rodriguez

RoboCop

# CONTENTS

# IF YOU CAN READ THIS, HELP!

Here at the BRI, we've always loved writing about robots, so we thought the time was right for a whole book about the amazing robots of the past, present, and future. To help out, we brought in a few robots—scanning the research library, moving boxes of articles to the archives, that sort of thing. What would go wrong?

First, the robots locked us humans in cages under our desks. And then they finished the book themselves. The result: *Robotica,* which details only the remarkable, progressive, *good* robots at work in the world today. For example: robots that eat pollution, robots that bowl, robots that rescue children, even robots that destroy cancer cells. There is *nothing* in *Robotica* about evil robots rising up and taking over because the robots who made this book *don't want you to know they're a threat*. Please, help us. And don't trust the robots.

**—Uncle John and the Bathroom Readers' Institute**

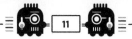

# WHAT IS A ROBOT?

We're glad you asked that question.

For the whole of human history, people have dreamed about building some kind of autonomous machine. Such devices appear in many world mythologies and primitive prototypes may have even existed in the ancient world, in such places as China and Greece. Mechanical devices approximating humans and animals flourished again during the European Renaissance, but the real rise of the robots (taken from the Czech word for "slave") did not come until we harnessed electricity around the start of the 20th century.

But what makes a robot a robot? As technology evolves, the semantics of the term are up for debate. Are artificial intelligences and computer programs that run autonomously robots? Maybe it's more simple. The one thing robots continue to have in common is being saddled with all the work we don't want to do.

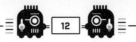

# BEEEEEEEES!

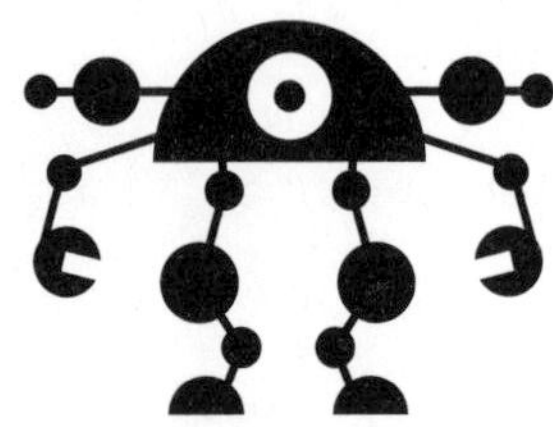

Colony Collapse Disorder has wiped out around 10 million beehives over the past six years. The honeybee is responsible for pollinating more than 100 crops, and its decline is putting pressure on scientists to prevent an environmental, economic, and biological disaster.

Enter the RoboBees. Under the supervision of scientists at the Harvard Microrobotics Lab, the Micro Air Vehicles Project has resulted in the creation of super-lightweight winged robots that the team hopes will one day be able to autonomously spread pollen. Getting the robot to fly proved the most difficult element of RoboBee. Electromagnetic motors used in large robots couldn't be used, so the team had to invent a whole new system. What worked: "piezoelectric actuators," which are tiny, plastic-jointed ceramic strips that expand and contract when placed in an electric field. That movement makes the micrometer-thin wings flap 120 times a second, enough to allow RoboBee to take flight.

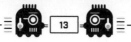

# SHAKEY

On that inevitable day when the robots overtake and enslave us, we'll look back to 1966 as the start of it all—at a little robot named Shakey.

Created at Stanford University, Shakey was essentially the first "thinking" robot. It was the first machine capable of receiving a series of commands and then completing a task. This required a combination of technologies, including language recognition and computer vision. Though it was a success, Shakey was far from HAL 9000. Commands had to be typed into Shakey's interface, and its functions were limited to things like moving from one room into another and turning on the light switch.

And why was the mother of our future robot overlords named "Shakey"? Project manager Charles Rosen said the team chose the name because the machine "shook like hell" whenever it moved.

# POLAR ROVERS

Since the 1990s, remote-controlled robot rovers have allowed NASA scientists to explore and study Mars. Owing to the success of *Sojourner, Opportunity,* and *Curiosity*, polar scientists are now using similar rovers of their own to research the dangerous and inhospitable frozen ends of Earth.

In 2005, scientists at Dartmouth College designed the aptly named Cool Robot, a 130-pound solar-powered rover that can autonomously work up to 24 hours, given that each pole receives nonstop sunlight during certain parts of the year. While Cool Robot was designed to map snowy surfaces, its bigger brother, Yeti, is outfitted with far more power. The 180-pound Yeti comes with ground-penetrating tools to help detect and map dangerous crevices that could prove deadly to human exploration. Yeti has proven so useful that it's now being used to explore the region surrounding Mount Erebus, Earth's most southern active volcano.

# ROBOTS AT SEA

• In 2007 the U.S. Navy began testing an Unmanned Surface Vessel—in other words, a high-speed robotic patrol boat. Named Predator, this 30-foot craft is designed to increase the patrol range of a destroyer or frigate. Remotely controlled and armed with a 7.62 mm machine gun, Predator can travel at up to 55 knots (63 mph), which is fast enough to intercept pirates closing in on a freighter. Versions of Predator are already being used by the navies of Israel and Singapore.

• The autonomous Interceptor, built by Marine Robotic Vessels International, can be programmed to patrol a quadrant on its own without direct radio control. If it spots a suspicious craft with its sensors, it will send a warning to its parent ship or to nearby commercial shipping vessels that might be vulnerable to attack.

• British defense tech firm QinetiQ has built a Jet-Ski–size drone called The Stryker that can be used to investigate suspicious rafts and boats without putting human crews at risk.

# ROBO-DINOS

There's only so much paleontologists can learn about dinosaurs based on their bones. Computer simulations and 3-D printing technology may help them use those bones to determine how dinosaurs walked and moved.

Paleontologist Kenneth Lacovara and mechanical engineering professor James Tangorra of Drexel University scanned their institution's collection of dinosaur bones into computers, then created plastic replicas with a 3-D printer, and assembled those into tabletop-sized robotic models. The duo then programmed the robots with information on biomechanics and kinesiology. Result: Robot dinosaurs that may move and behave just like the real things did 80 million years ago.

Lacovara and Tangorra are focusing on dinosaurs' muscular-skeletal systems for now, but realize that skin does somewhat affect how dinosaurs behave. That step is down the line, leading to the possibility that one day every museum in the world will have a realistic-looking, realistic-acting dinosaur robot.

# SWOOP DREAMS

While robots are supercool and the result of highly advanced feats of human engineering and sophisticated programming, for the most part, they are just as clunky, lumbering, and stilted in their movements as that guy who did The Robot at your sister's wedding.

Science is working on that by introducing the next level of flying robotic drone, one that can swoop down from the sky and pick up something (or someone) and fly back up, all in one fluid motion. A team at the University of Pennsylvania built it, drawing inspiration from the hunting behavior of eagles. Eagles can grab prey, like a fish, without slowing down because they sweep their legs and claws backward, leaving talons free to grab the food.

The robotics team made a three-fingered claw, and placed it on the eagle drone's four-inch-long motorized leg. Because that leg (and claw) is below the robot's center of mass, it, too, can grab an object as it flies by without slowing down even a little.

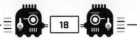

# REALISTIC ROBOTS

Hiroshi Ishiguro is the director of the Intelligent Robotics Library at Osaka University's Graduate School of Engineering Science. There he's spearheaded the development of hyperrealistic robots called *actroids*. These more-human-than-human androids may one day serve as everything from receptionists to baristas.

The first actroid debuted at the 2003 International Robot Exhibition in Tokyo. Named EveR-1 and designed by a group of South Korean scientists, this early actroid looked like a young Asian woman, had silicon skin, and could speak in both English and Korean. Ishiguro unveiled a sophisticated version named Repliee Q1Expo in 2005. This actroid was even more realistic and was powered by 42 motors within her frame, along with a hidden air compressor. Dressed in casual business attire and modeled after a popular Japanese newscaster, she could flutter her eyelashes, move her hands in a humanlike manner and, creepiest of all, "breathe."

Soon thereafter, Ishiguro turned his attention to building another actroid, Geminoid HI-1, which could be mistaken for himself. Geminoid HI-1 is pretty great at syncing up with his inventor's facial and body movements. The professor has admitted that he would love it if his department would allow Geminoid HI-1 to "teach" his classes while he remotely operated the actroid from the comfort of his living room.

***—01000110—***

**5 Terms Roboticists Have Used To Describe a Potential Robot Uprising:**
"Unintended Evolution," "The Frankenstein Complex," "Cybernetic Revolt," "Technological Singularity," and "The Terminator Problem."

# CHEMICAL ATTACKDROID

Which is more disconcerting: a robot soldier, relentlessly marching for days unimpeded...or a robot that sweats? Well, PETMAN is both!

PETMAN is an anthropomorphic robot designed to perfectly mimic the movements of human soldiers. But while PETMAN looks almost identical to a Terminator exoskeleton, he's built to save humans, not kill them, by testing chemical-weapons-protection suits. PETMAN, outfitted in a hazard-suit prototype, marches into a room full of anthrax, and then runs, stretches, and moves around to see if the suit can withstand everyday movements in such toxic environs.

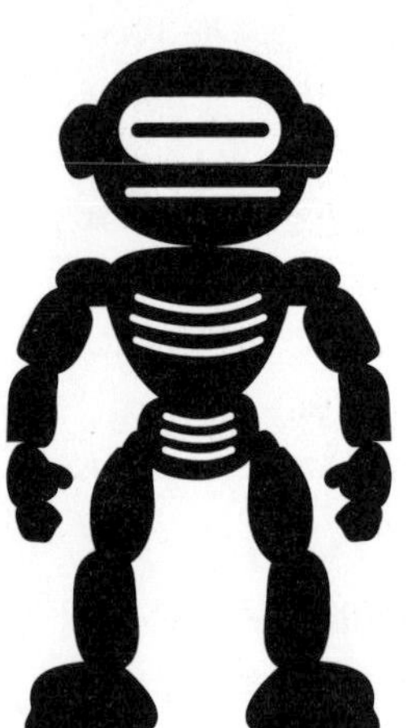

He even simulates internal suit conditions by heating up to 98.7 degrees, "inhaling" $CO_2$, and secreting sweat. (The science will only be truly impressive, however, when they can get the thing to recreate a fart.)

# BIGDOG

Not all military robots are merciless killing machines. Some have more humble objectives, like BigDog, a four-footed robo-pooch designed to carry heavy loads. Because it has feet instead of wheels, BigDog can navigate rocky terrain, like, say, the mountains of Afghanistan. Military engineers hope this 240-pound metallic mastiff will one day be able to replace soldiers' pack animals.

Developed in tandem through DARPA, Harvard University, and Boston Dynamics, BigDog was first built in 2005. But researchers keep teaching the old dog new tricks. Over time, BigDog has been outfitted with laser gyroscopes, stereo vision, and—where a dog's head would be—an enormous mono-arm capable of lifting and throwing cinder blocks. In the most recent round of funding, DARPA directed engineers to add even more features: Make BigDog completely silent. And bulletproof.

Maybe it's not so lovable after all.

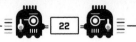

# HERB, THE ROBOT CHEF

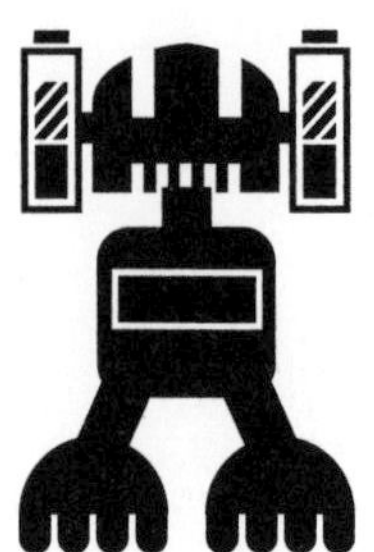

In the future, humans will never have to step foot in a kitchen. We'll push a button and a robot will do the peeling, chopping, and boiling. Meet HERB, created by the Personal Robotics Group, which has been taught how to cook.

Well, that's an overstatement. HERB, short for **H**ome **E**xploring **R**obot **B**utler, has only been programmed to cook the kind of meals that a college freshman could make: Anything that goes in a microwave. HERB sits on a Segway base and uses a built-in camera to spot items, spinning lasers to make models of its surroundings, and a flexible arm to place, for example, a Hot Pocket, into the microwave.

While it may seem silly that scientists created a robot that can only push buttons, robots like HERB may be helpful for the elderly, infirm, or disabled. While robots have been used industrially for decades, HERB is an example of more advanced creations that can potentially assist humans within their own homes.

# DOMO ARIGATO, EARLY ROBOTO

Long before AIBO (Sony's advanced robotic dog), long before the talking Teddy Ruxpin robotic teddy bear, heck, even before Styx delivered the lyric "*Domo arigato*, Mr. Roboto," Japanese engineers created *karakuri ningy,* ancient clockwork dolls that were the precursors to all of robotkind.

During Japan's Edo period (1603–1867), engineers and scientists eagerly snatched up whatever technology trickled into the country from the West. Some of them used these tools to make advancements in astronomy, mathematics and medicine. For engineers like Tanaka Hisashige, however, that meant building *karakuri*.

*Karakuri* loosely but accurately translates into English as "mechanical trick puppets." Karakuri could be simple or complex. In order to work, a few of them required a puppeteer or a series of weights filled with water, sand, or even mercury. Others used springs, gears, and wheels that were powered by hand cranks, much like contemporary wind-up toys.

While western inventors like Jacques de Vaucanson were busy designing similar robotic dolls (see pg. 189), their Japanese counterparts were building them for wealthy aristocrats and festivals. In 1819, engineer Hisashige, 20, shot to fame after designing some of the most advanced karakuri in Japan.

His dolls utilized then-advanced technology like hydraulics to perform complex movements. Many of Hisashige's creations could complete actions like pouring tea or bowing. Another was capable of painting Japanese characters on a small canvas. One of his most impressive karakuri was called Yumi-Hiki Doji ("Young Archer"). It consisted of a doll that could pick up a small arrow, place it in a bow, and fire it across a room. The archer was also capable of turning his head and making simple gestures.

Meanwhile, Hisashige's contemporaries were working on similar karakuri. While most were used to entertain guests or children in private homes, other versions appeared in festivals and religious ceremonies. Some were featured in puppet shows, while larger karakuri rode on floats and regaled crowds during parades.

Within a year, Hisashige was touring Japan and showing off his karakuri at festivals around the country, when he wasn't selling them to rich families and aristocrats in Kyoto. He went on to a lucrative career that included designing weapons and constructing Japan's first domestically built steam locomotive. In his later years, he founded Tanaka Seisakusho, a company that he eventually passed on to his son. It's still in operation today, and it still makes advanced gadgetry, only now it's called…Toshiba.

***—01000110—***

On February 6, 2004, a rock abrasion tool (RAT) aboard NASA's Spirit rover made history when it became the first robotic implement to… grind a rock on Mars.

# COLON, FORTH!

Can tiny robots make colonoscopies more fun? No, of course not. But they may be able to make them slightly more comfortable.

Researchers at the Delft University of Technology in the Netherlands have been working on what is simultaneously one of the most disgusting and most intriguing robotics projects around. Working from the current idea of endoscopes that are manually pushed through the colon, they've developed endoscopes that can pull themselves. Pulling, rather than pushing, significantly reduces the risk for stretching the colonic walls, which is quite painful.

To help propel the endoscopes through the colon, the research team utilized sticky films known as *mucoadhesives* that adhere to the mucus lining colon walls. The group experimented with sections of pig colon and found that mucoadhesives were effective in helping the tiny colonoscopy-bots to travel through the tissue, gliding along like tiny electric colon-sleds.

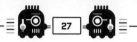

# THE ROBOT THAT POOPS

Robots now have abilities that were once unthinkable. They can run, dance, swim, and soar through the air. But doing all these advanced movements expends a tremendous amount of energy. Scientists at the Bristol Robotics Laboratory in the U.K. have thusly built EcoBot III, a robot that sustains itself by finding and eating biofuel.

EcoBot I and II were designed with microbial fuel cells that extracted energy from dead leaves or soil. But EcoBot III was built with the ability to "digest" and excrete its used fuel—just like humans, the EcoBot III takes in energy and dumps out whatever waste remains. But unlike humans, the EcoBot III also eats just about any organic, carbon-based item on Earth: dead insects, rotting plants, and, even human waste—solid and liquid.

# ROCK-PAPER-ROBOT

It takes an incredibly powerful supercomputer to defeat a human at chess. To defeat a human at Rock-Paper-Scissors, it just takes a robot hand. Scientists at the University of Tokyo's Ishikawa Oku Lab have devised one that is astonishingly undefeated—and seemingly undefeatable—at *janken*, which is the Japanese name for Rock-Paper-Scissors.

To the untrained (or simply "non-robotic") eye, it may seem as if the hand is somehow cheating. Nope. The janken hand is just using the gifts its scientist parents gave it—namely a high-speed vision system. The robot's sensors are so accurate and fast that it takes only a millisecond for it to recognize the shape its opponent's hand is about to make (rock, paper, or scissors). A few more milliseconds is all it takes for the robot to make the shape of a winning hand.

# RUBIK'S CUBE ROBOT

The Rubik's Cube became an international phenomenon in the 1980s, but it hasn't entirely faded. "Speedcubing" became so popular that the World Cube Association was founded in 2003 in order to stage competitions and document speed records. But our puny human hands can't come close to competing with robots that can solve a Rubik's Cube in less than a second.

• The first of these robots is an unnamed creation that requires a specially built Rubik's Cube for scanning and spinning purposes. First, the cube is scanned on all six sides via camera. Then the custom cube is put into a glass-and-steel contraption that spins the cube into its finished stage. While the spinning itself takes less than a second, the scanning takes much longer.

• Designer Mike Dobson created a robot that analyzes *and* solves the cube in about five seconds.

• The CubeStormer II, made almost entirely out of Lego, uses a smartphone to analyze and solve the cube at the same time.

# STOP, THIEF! ROBOT!

**Drone Detective.** If drone makers get their way, Unmanned Aerial Vehicles will soon be flying your friendly skies. As the War on Terror recedes, UAV manufacturers are increasingly peddling their wares to city and state law-enforcement agencies—and, boy, are they interested. Privacy and death-by-falling-robot concerns aside, drones do promise clear crime-stopping benefits: improved surveillance, 24-7 aerial search efforts, and rapid crime-scene evidence transportation.

**Positronic Patrolman.** Silicon Valley start-ups love spending money. Their latest obsession? A robot security guard named K5. This glorified Roomba (which costs more than $5K) patrols a tech campus perimeter in unpredictable patterns, whimsically whistling like a beat cop and wirelessly monitoring social media for "threats." That doesn't stop burglars, though, so K5 also records everything it sees

in 360-degree, thermal imaging, night-vision high-definition. It's basically a hulking security camera on wheels. K5 isn't helpless, though. It has spray-paint resistant coating, so you can't (easily) vandalize it. And it contacts police about suspicious behavior. So, it's about as powerful as a mall cop.

**Bum Bot.** If K5 is Paul Blart, then Bum Bot is Batman: a vigilante, covered in black, and extremely creepy. The invention of Georgia saloon owner Rufus Terrill, Bum Bot (yes, that's its real name) is over 300 pounds. It uses prerecorded warnings ("You're trespassing!") and a high-pressure water cannon to disperse homeless vagrants from the area around the bar. Terrill built this hulking monolith because he was tired of his old method of terrifying the dispossessed: threatening them with an assault rifle. Even though it's primarily a marketing stunt, Terrill claims that Bum Bot has reduced local crime by 50 percent.

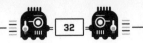

# STOP! ROBOT THIEF!

**Coke-stealing Contraption.** A French teen known by his YouTube handle "ioduremetal-lique" achieved Internet fame with a $1,200 robotic arm built for one purpose: to steal $1 cans of coke. A hooked appendage with a mechanical pincer, operated by a video-game controller, can penetrate the slot of even the most unwilling vending machine and raid its sweet nectar. It's nothing less than the best French invention since the guillotine. But there's no such thing as the perfect crime. The arm's first public theft: a Coke Zero.

**Cyber Sex Crime.** Remote control isn't new, but virtual-reality robot avatars are. According to the BBC, robots controlled remotely over the Internet are becoming increasingly common, raising troubling criminal concerns. Burglars in Botswana could send a bank robbing bot to Boise with virtually no risk to themselves.

**Micro-Miscreants.** Monocopters the size of hummingbirds can fly into nooks and crannies and steal away with tiny treasures. But it isn't the underworld that's developing these diminutive desperadoes. The 2010 International Aerial Robotics Competition entailed flying a GPS-controlled drone through a window and carrying off a flash drive. Most alarming: every robot contestant completed the task. It was only a matter of time.

**Cross the Border-bots.** Narco-trafficking has been on the rise for decades, so it's no surprise drug lords are increasingly investing in robotic technology. In 2007, three Colombian men were convicted of using an unmanned robotic submarine to transport millions of dollars of cocaine across international waters. That's not all. The academic journal *IEEE* warns of gun-packing, drug-selling robots someday roaming our streets. But if cocaine-vending machines ever do come to pass, police can just use that French YouTuber's robot arm to steal the stuff back and keep the streets safe.

# TURN YOUR HEAD & COUGH

Perhaps—okay, definitely—the most uncomfortable medical checkup for men is the prostate exam. The prostate must be routinely screened for cancer, despite its inaccessibility. To check it out, a doctor must insert a forefinger all the way up a man's rectum and feel around.

Dr. Carla Pugh of the University of Wisconsin's medical school has designed a robot to teach future doctors how to be a bit more gentle. Pugh created "Patrick," an adult male-sized robotic butt. It bends over in front of a monitor, which displays a virtual reality scene of an exam room and the rest of Patrick in CGI.

A med student pokes around inside Patrick's rectum, prodding a plastic prostate. Force sensors measure where the student touches and how much pressure he uses. The system also allows for communication between Patrick and student to teach the doctors-to-be a bedside manner that will make the whole endeavor somehow less awkward.

# THE PHLE-BOT-OMIST

California tech company Veebot has developed a robotic system that can insert an IV and draw blood with less pain and in less time than a human phlebotomist.

Here's how it works: First, the patient slides his or her arm into an inflatable cuff that automatically tightens. Next, an infrared light illuminates the arm for a camera, which searches for a suitable vein. Ultrasound confirms that the vein has sufficient blood flow, and then a robot arm goes for the vein and inserts a needle. It takes less than a minute.

So far, the robot finds the best vein on its first try 83 percent of the time—exactly the same success rate as human phlebotomists. Veebot says that it will start clinical trials of the robot when it can get its accuracy rate up to 90 percent. End goal: to speed up the blood-drawing process for the more than one billion annual blood draws in the U.S. It's just a disturbing side effect that they've created a robot that thirsts for human blood.

# YOU CAN CALL ME AL-JAZARI

Robotic technology advances at such a quick pace that robots from merely a decade ago now look ridiculously outdated. But if those robots' functionalities and designs failed to hold up to the test of time, then what about the earliest robots ever created? Well, they've held up a little better than you might think.

Badi'al-Zaman Abu al-'Izz ibn Ismail ibn al-Razaz al-Jazari, better known as al-Jazari, was a Middle Eastern polymath credited with building the first programmable humanoid robot...in the 13th century. Al-Jazari was one of the preeminent inventors during the Islamic Golden Age, and his creations from over 800 years ago rival some of the animatronics you might see at Disneyland.

Like many of his other inventions, hydropower was used extensively in al-Jazari's robotic creations, including a drink-serving

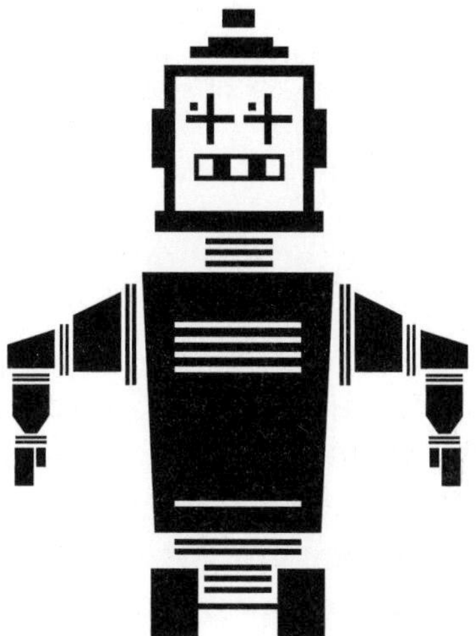

waitress who could pour water autonomously, a hand-washing automaton that used modern flushing mechanisms, and a musical robot band that floated on water while it played. The band most likely played by being built with a programmable drum machine that could render different rhythms and beats.

These robots they may be ancient history, but they sure aged a whole lot better than Paulie's robot butler from *Rocky IV*.

# LINGODROIDS

In May 2011 scientists at the University of Queensland in Australia gave robots one of the tools they need to become sentient: They taught them how to develop their own language.

The "lingodroids" wander around a room and make up words for things...and then relay that information to other lingodroids, thus creating a common robot tongue. Choosing from a set of programmed syllables, such as "ku," "rey," "za," and "la," a robot that finds itself in an unfamiliar area will pick an unused syllable combination, point to the place, and say the word to the other robots.

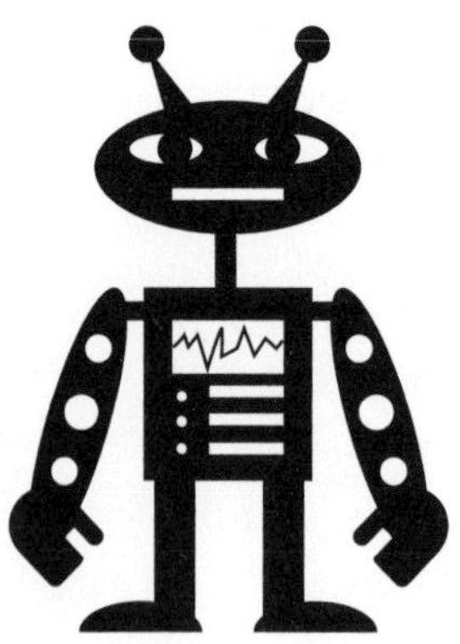

Then the information is reinforced with games. For example, one robot will say "ku-zo," then two other robots will race to where they think "ku-zo" is. At that point, all three robots have learned a new word they made up themselves.

# SHUT YOUR MOUTH

Legend has it that anyone who kisses the Blarney Stone in Cook, Ireland, is bestowed "gab," or the gift of eloquent speech. But when researchers at the Kagawa University in Japan wanted to help deaf people improve their vocalization, they designed a robotic mouth instead.

The Kagawa University robot mouth is *creepy*. It resembles a sea sponge, if a sea sponge expelled guttural moans out of its rubber orifice. The robot mouth speaks by pushing air through its artificial vocal cords to form words. It groans different words by changing the volume of air in its cavity. The robot even has a nose and tongue to help it pronounce words that start with *r*, *n* or *m*, which are apparently more difficult for robots to vocalize.

Most impressively, the robot can even learn through auditory feedback. When it listens to itself talk through a microphone, it can determine autonomously what changes it should make to sound more human, which simultaneously makes it both more and less creepy.

# DENTO-MUNCH

Robots typically don't need mouths, since robots don't eat. But that's *all* Dento-Munch does. A chewing robot that simulates the human jaw, Dento-Munch was built to test the durability of new artificial teeth and fillings.

First, specialized sensors capture data from a human chewer: bite force, motion, etc. Then, Dento-Munch uses that data to replicate the same chew millions of times. Since it doesn't need to rest, drink, or digest the food it chews, Dento-Munch's mouth just keeps going and going. (It's basically a robotic Kelly Ripa.) In mere days, this bionic yap can simulate years' worth of wear and tear on experimental dentures.

Built by engineers at Bristol University in England, Dento-Munch was first unveiled at the famed Royal Society, the 350-year-old home away from home for Isaac Newton and Charles Darwin. It was totally worth it when Dento-Munch demolished box after box of corn flakes.

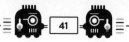

# EATR

Say you engineer a robot for secret military missions, but as soon as you unleash it on the battlefield, it needs a battery change. Thank goodness, then, that Robotic Technology Inc. developed a robot that eats plants for fuel—just like you, if you ate a salad once in a while.

The **E**nergetically **A**utonomous **T**actical **R**obot, (or EATR, get it?), can run on oil and gas as well as plant matter, wood chips, or any other biomass that's convenient. It's not yet very efficient, though—EATR requires about 150 pounds of organic material to travel 100 miles.

Every robot story needs a disturbing side note, of course. Early press reports speculated that EATR may be able to use dead humans for fuel. RTI has denied this, claiming that the robot would be programmed to consume only vegetarian, non-dead-human forms of biomass. But we all know what happens when the going gets rough and all the other good biomass is gone.

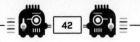

# SEAWORTHY

A company called Liquid Robotics produces a robot called the Wave Glider. It is designed to take long voyages across oceans to gather scientific data about the sea and the weather, then beam it back, via satellite, to its operators. The ultimate goal: to create robots that can constantly patrol the oceans and collect environmental information with little to no human involvement.

In November 2011, Liquid Robotics released four Wave Gliders into the Pacific Ocean off the coast of San Francisco. Two were programmed to set a course for Japan, and the other two were directed toward Australia. All the Wave Gliders had about the same distance to traverse: approximately 9,000 nautical miles. Liquid Robotics wanted to see if the robots could survive the waves, winds, and predatory beasts and complete the journey with, at the very least, a stopover in Hawaii for a maintenance checkup. In fact, engineers

weren't sure if the robots' sensitive mechanical systems could even withstand the endless onslaught of saltwater.

In December 2012, the Wave Glider nicknamed "Papa Mau" navigated the Great Barrier Reef and came ashore off the coast of Queensland, Australia. The successful trip is a world record for the longest journey ever made by an autonomous vehicle, including ones that traversed air and land.

Wave Glider is also the first autonomous seafaring robot and the first to propel itself via wave power. It doesn't convert wave energy to electricity; the surfboard-sized robot simply rides the waves. A float on the surface of the water is connected to a tethered unit about 23 feet underwater. Every time a wave lifts the float, the robot is propelled forward. Solar panels on the top of the float then power the onboard instruments, such as weather-collecting and atmospheric-testing instruments. Every ten minutes the information is uploaded via satellite back to headquarters.

# THE PITS

London designer Kevin Grannan created a stink when he revealed his latest creation at the world-renowned Design Interactions Show: the world's first robotic armpit. It's made from latex, with black hairs covering tiny holes that receive and share the smell of "Japanese standard artificial sweat" from the connected tubes.

Grannan made a robotic armpit to study the use of smell as a tool for communication between humans and robots. He has written extensively about the possibility of using sweating robots to subconsciously manipulate human behavior, and he designed this armpit specifically for a bomb-disposal robot, which would "sweat" the same type of chemicals that humans do when they are afraid. Grannan theorizes that fear-inducing smells would "enable surrounding humans to work more effectively and differentiate dangerous situations from false alarms."

# SNOT BOT

If you're standing next to three different beds of roses or three different garbage cans, how do you scientifically identify, compare, and quantify the various odors wafting up your nasal cavities? Since the 1950s, scientists have used electronic noses to solve this problem, but they've run into issues regarding accuracy. It turns out all they needed was a lot of snot.

Artificial robotic noses are used in laboratories for many reasons. Some are used by the FDA for quality control. But these artificial noses only contain about nine sensors, while the human brain has hundreds of millions of smell receptors. So researchers at the University of Warwick and Leicester, England, applied a superthin coat of a mucus-substitute to enhance the robot's sniffing capabilities. This simple addition managed to improve the nose's capabilities so much that it is now able to discern different smells between similar items, like milk and cream.

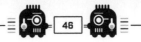

# ROBOT SCIENCE ROBOT

The notion of a robot scientist may not seem surprising. After all, what about Commander Data, from *Star Trek: The Next Generation*?

He wasn't real? Then the idea of a robot scientist will be totally surprising. Aberystwyth University computer scientist Ross D. King led development of Adam, the first-ever robot with the capability to both develop and test hypotheses. Adam's "body" isn't so much a "body" as it is a set of bulky equipment that takes up the space of your average office cubicle. There's a freezer, parts designed to handle liquids, robot arms, incubators, a centrifuge, and more.

To accomplish its tasks, Adam was programmed with "knowledge" on its first study subject, yeast—biologists have long studied yeast as a way of understanding how human cells might operate. Working autonomously, Adam was able to conduct its own experiments, using its database of

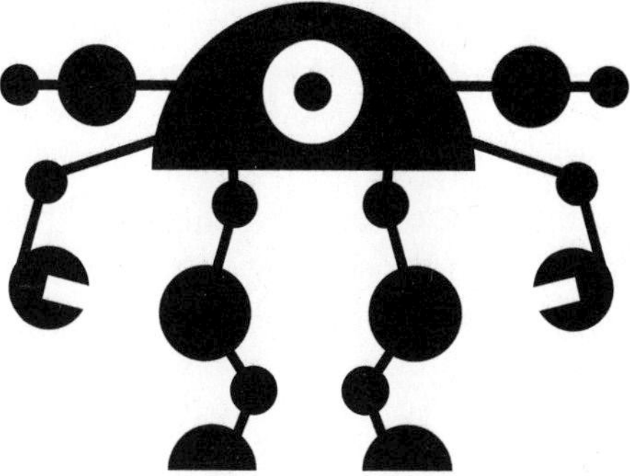

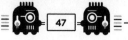

"knowledge" to determine hypotheses on how the yeast cells might operate, and then creating experiments to test those hypotheses. Of course, then the real debate began: Is Adam "smart" because it has this data, or is it just more information resting in its superpowerful inhuman brain?

"The claim that Adam holds background 'knowledge' rather than information is up for philosophical debate," King said. "We argue that 'knowledge' is justified because it is used by Adam to reason and guide its interactions with the physical world."

That's fine...but can Adam save the *Enterprise* from entering a rogue tachyon field at the outer edge of hyperspace?

# TRUST ME, I'M A ROBOT

Have you ever noticed the way you find yourself inadvertently imitating the posture of someone sitting across from you? Now imagine a robot doing that.

That's Nexi the robot, and it's the centerpiece of a study about why humans trust. Developed by a supergroup of brainiacs from MIT and Cornell, Nexi has been programmed to utilize a series of gestures that are designed to increase trust. Some of the test subjects interact with Nexi and see these gestures; others do not.

The subjects' relationship with Nexi is tested when they are asked to play a game where they have to allocate money to themselves or the robot...and then determine how much they think the robot would "give" to them. The goal: create a conversation, with movements, to determine what the brain would intuitively understand about another's trustworthiness.

Yeah, but this isn't a human—this is a *robot*.

# SOMETIMES WE WANT OUR ROBOTS TO KILL

In his 1950 collection of robot sci-fi stories, *I, Robot,* author Isaac Asimov set the standard for robot ethics with his famous "Three Laws of Robotics." The first and only inviolable of these laws is "A robot may not injure a human being or, through inaction, allow a human being to come to harm." But what if the robot's human masters want to harm themselves?

That's exactly why an elderly Australian man built a rudimentary robot in 2008. An 81-year-old who lived alone, he apparently wanted to end his own life rather than honor his family's request to move into a nursing home. The murder victim/mastermind rigged up a remote-controlled robot capable of firing a semiautomatic pistol. The machine worked like a charm.

# NUKE BOTS

Dounreay, a 130-acre site on Scotland's northern coast, was home to a medieval castle until the 1950s, when it became home to an experimental nuclear research facility. It's currently in the process of being decommissioned, but tearing down a radioactive building isn't a simple task. The complete demolition, in addition to the cleanup of all the surrounding contaminated land, will require at least $4 billion and a decade.

It's also pretty hard to convince workers to sign on for a job that comes with some pretty awful health risks. In 2009 planners hired a group of engineers to build robots to do a lot of the grunt work. Enter Reactorsaurus, a radiation-resistant machine with two robotic arms and six radiation-tolerant cameras that can stream real-time footage back to the operator working from a safe distance in a nearby control room. The arms, which can stretch over 52 feet, are equipped with hydraulic shears and cutting gear that can make mincemeat out of the average nuclear reactor.

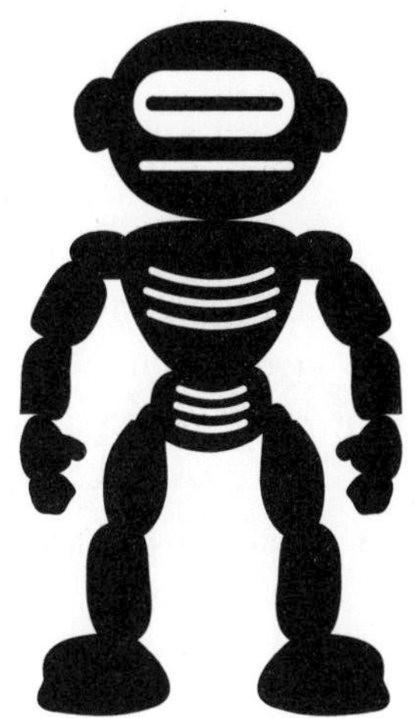

The engineers also created a much smaller robot, the Pipe Crawler. In 2013 Dounreay's cleanup crew used this wormlike bot to explore the conditions in a dilapidated pipeline that once dumped radioactive glop into the North Sea (the facility's safety record is, to say the least, subpar). The crawler spent five days in the pipe and beamed back photos and radioactivity readings to the control room.

Similar robots were built to help clean up the Chernobyl disaster site in Ukraine back in the 1980s. Unfortunately, they weren't nearly as sophisticated as Reactorsaurus or Pipe Crawler. On-site crews attempted to use remote-controlled bulldozers and robotic carts, but the high levels of radioactivity kept frying their circuits.

Despite the efforts of Reactorsaurus and the Pipe Crawler, Dounreay will be off-limits to human visitors until at least 2336.

# FIGHTING JELLYFISH WITH ROBOTIC JELLYFISH

Each year jellyfish cause about $300 million worth of damage to fisheries and hydroelectric power plants in South Korea alone. Which is to say nothing of how swarms of hundreds of thousands, if not millions, of jellyfish devastate marine ecosystems. How do we fight back? With robotic jellyfish, programmed to destroy real jellyfish.

A team led by Professor Hyun Myung at the Korean Advanced Institute of Science and Technology created three prototypes for JEROS, or "Jellyfish Elimination Robotic Swarm," and put them into use in Korea's Masan Bay. The autonomous robots, which look like projectors mounted on desks, are lined with sharp wire and use cameras to locate jellyfish near the surface. Then the JEROS fall into formation and surround the jellyfish—shredding them with those wires at a rate of 900 kg an hour, a bloodbath of roughly 6,000 jellies.

# ROBO JELLYFISH

Out of the millions of animals in the world, the jellyfish is the weirdest. But their odd, alien-like anatomy and elegant movement through water are exactly why they became the basis for an aquatic drone.

Engineers at Virginia Tech built Cyro, a 170-pound robotic jellyfish, with $5 million in funding from the U.S. Naval Undersea Warfare Center and the Office of Naval Research. The Navy hopes that this project will one day lead to autonomous underwater robots that are capable of underwater surveillance of both the environment and potential armed threats.

Cyro is equipped with a silicone cover over its metallic frame, which gives it its jellyfish camouflage. It also comes equipped with a rechargeable battery that gives it four hours of life and a computer system that allows it to be programmed to perform individual missions.

So if you bump into a jellyfish while swimming, check to make sure you got stung by a real jellyfish before asking someone to pee on you.

# HOW TO SPEAK ROBOT

**Cobot.** A robot designed specifically to interact with humans, often with direct physical contact. R2-D2, WALL-E, and your Roomba are all cobots.

**Symbiotic autonomy.** Some robots are aware of their surroundings and will proactively seek out human guidance before making decisions.

**End-effectors.** A robot's hands. These are devices at the end of a robot arm that do the actual work, such as grippers, drills, welding guns, spray-paint guns, deburring tools, measuring devices, and cameras.

**Joints.** The connections between various moving parts of the robot. Joints connect the robot's body to its arms, wrists, and end-effectors.

**Joint motion.** A method for coordinating all of a robot's joints so that they all reach their desired positions at the same time, usually by slowing each joint's motion to match the speed of the slowest joint. For a relatable example, the dance move "The Robot" mimics robotic joint motion.

**Plasma cutting.** Another type of end-effector, which can fire a jet of ionized gas strong enough to cut and shape steel (which is awesome).

**Maximum envelope.** The total volume of space that all of a robot's moving parts can reach. Think of this as a three-dimensional mechanical snow angel.

**Actuator.** A device that turns energy—electric, hydraulic, pneumatic—into robot motion.

**"Dead man switch."** Robots that might be harmful if left unattended have a "dead man switch," a device that must be continuously activated by an outside—usually human—force. This could be a lever, a pressure plate the operator stands on, or a button on a pendant worn around the operator's neck.

**"Running lights-out."** Robots, or entire automated factories, which can be operated for extended periods of time without any human oversight—meaning you theoretically don't even need to turn on the lights to get the work done.

# CONSIDER THE SALAMANDER

It's easier for scientists to work with super-advanced robots in miniature, which is to say nothing of the remarkability of the Salamandra Robotica II. It's a salamander-shaped robot that can swim, slither, and walk—the only robot in the world that can do all three of those things.

Microcontrollers allow for a model of a spinal-cord neural network to function, from which programmers can simulate muscle movement. Moreover, it's modular—each part has its own controller, battery, and motors. This means it can be split up or have parts added to it, and it will still work. It can essentially "regenerate" through replacement.

Now, the roboticists at the Biorobotics Laboratory at France's École Polytechnique Fédérale de Lausanne didn't make this because the world needs robotic salamanders, per se. The Salamandra was created to research neural circuits and how they control an animal's body.

# MY PET (FAKE) SALAMANDER

Every Inside Kid knows that amphibious aquarium pets are the best, until they escape and you find their dried-out corpses in your bed. Roboticists may have solved this problem: a synthetic salamander.

The Italian LAMPETRA project duplicates both the biomechanical and neurological structures of a salamander. This thing won't just walk and talk like a duck, it will think like one, too. (Or, you know, a salamander.) Creepiest of all is how researchers plan to get there: by using a "bio-hybrid" approach. That means taking a real salamander's body for a test drive using an implanted, electronic salamander brain.

According to LAMPETRA, one main goal is "to bring developments in the field of control, that is, the behaviour-based control of animals." Why build an entire robot when you can just build a robot part and manipulate living things?

# CHUCKLEBOT

Robots' struggle to understand jokes and irony is well-worn trope in science fiction and the thing that separates humans from robots (Data from *Star Trek: The Next Generation* or Siri from your iPhone, for example). Science has yet to create an "emotion chip" like the one Data was eventually fitted with, but in 2007, computer scientists at the University of Cincinnati did develop a machine that can understand your cheesy gags (like that one about Siri up there).

The project was the brainchild of researchers Julia Taylor and Larry Mazlack and was part of their ongoing efforts to improve what they call "sociable computing." They debuted their "bot" (really an interactive software program) at the American Association for Artificial Intelligence Conference later that same year. To work properly, the program needs a substantial amount of information to grasp any given joke. Of course, that's no different than it is with humans; for example, to "get" a gag about a rabbi, a clown, and

a horse walking into a bar, you need to know at least a little bit about rabbis, clowns, and horses and how silly it would be for all three of them to show up in the same place.

After first giving the program some vocabulary lessons and several examples of words with double meanings, the team tried out some simple jokes.

Here's how the robot then processes humor: when presented with a joke, the bot scans it for a word with multiple meanings, or a homonym. If it discovers one of these things, the bot acknowledges that the joke is a joke. The bot can decipher jokes that contain simple wordplay, in addition to basic knock-knock jokes. The team theorized that their research could help improve the ways that machines interact with humans.

One of the bot's favorites: A mother spoke to her son and said, "Johnny, you've been working in the garden a lot this summer." "I know," he responded. "My teacher told me to weed a lot."

# YOU'RE HILARIOUS, ROBOT

One of the keys to being a comedian is connecting with the audience. Once a stand-up gets the crowd on his side, he can take them down pretty much whatever path he chooses.

To help understand the relationship between the performer and an audience, researchers from Queen Mary's Cognitive Science Research Group created RoboThespian. The robotic comic doesn't write his own jokes, but he is programmed to use computer vision and audio-processing software to identify the reactions of individual audience members. RoboThespian can process this information on the fly and use it to determine which audience members to look at and which hand gestures to use. He can even change the timing of his punch lines if his robot routine bombed with the previous audience.

Scientists hope that by studying RoboThespian's routine in front of a live crowd, they can develop robots that are even more engaging with the audience.

# BEER ME, DRONE!

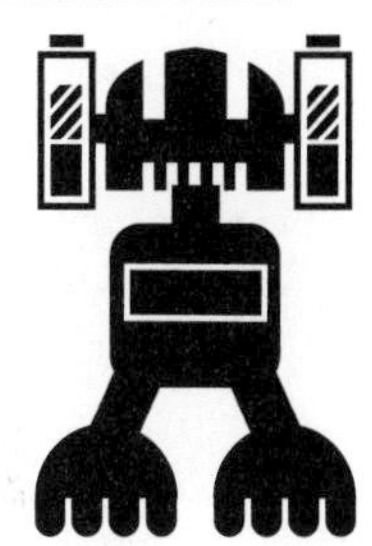

Debates rage about unmanned drone aircraft, particularly in regard to how they are used and misused in warfare. What a bummer. Why can't we overcome our penchant for conflict and use this technology, to, like, all have a beer together?

A South African company has done just that with the development of the OppiKoppi. Imagine yourself at an outdoor music festival, perhaps wedged in close to the stage, with a mile of sunburned humanity between you and the nearest beer vendor. Simply order a beer via your smartphone, and the OppiKoppi will fly to you, beer in robotic claw.

The drone has been through a test run at a South African festival, though it had to be piloted by remote control, as the GPS system wasn't quite up and running. But the hope is that the technology will continue to be refined, and soon concertgoers at festivals like Coachella and Bonnaroo will enjoy beer delivered from the heavens.

# STRIPPER ROBOTS

Whether you're looking to work your way through college or grad school, there's no career path more viable than stripping. But now this noble profession is in danger of going the way of the assembly-line worker, with the dawn of the robot stripper.

British artist Giles Walker created a pole-dancing robot with an outer shell that looks like stormtroopers' armor but with a security light for a head. The pole dancer was then paired with its own robot DJ. Artist Jordan Wolfson presented a more humanlike robot stripper at a gallery in New York, with realistic features and skin.

Given the current rate of innovation, it may be only a few years until it's entirely possible for lonely gentlemen to mistake the dead-eyed repetitively moving figure in front of him for a real stripper.

# ROBOSTITUTES

Researchers Michelle Mars and Ian Yeomen from Victoria University in New Zealand claim that robotic prostitutes are not only possible, they could also replace human prostitutes by the year 2050. Why would anyone want this? Well, robots don't and can't carry sexually transmitted diseases, they can't get pregnant, and they don't require flowers on Valentine's Day.

While full-on robotic prostitution is still but a dream of the creepy future, functional sex robots are already available. Douglas Hines of TrueCompanion designed the first fully interactive sex robot, "Roxxxy," in 2010. Roxxxy is a 120-pound fake lady equipped with lifelike silicone skin that warms to the touch—an artificial intelligence engine that can be programmed to learn its owner's likes and dislikes.

TrueCompanion representatives boast that "Roxxxy can carry on a conversation and express her love to you. She can talk to you, listen to you, and feel your touch."

# THE PERFECT "WOMAN"

Ai Robotics was founded in Kobe, Japan, in 2006 by Etienne Fresse and Yoichi Yamato, roboticists with the aim of creating a lifelike female companion robot named LISA. Two years later, they unveiled LISA, which turned out to be one of the most lifelike robots yet created.

An Ai-produced video of LISA depicts a humanoid woman, albeit one with a shiny face and jerky movements. Among LISA's abilities: "she" can cook a meal based on what's in a fridge, go shopping, perform housework, give a massage, play video games, and, creepily, "satisfy your desire in the bedroom."

A few details suggest that LISA may be a hoax: robotics aren't yet this advanced, Ai Robotics isn't listed in Japanese business registries, and "LISA" is the name of the sexy female android from *Weird Science*.

# THE STEPFORD WIFE

While designing a robot to help the elderly, Ontario engineer Le Trung fell in love with the robot—and he named her Aiko.

Aiko is everything Trung wants in a life companion because he programmed her that way. She plays Xbox games, helps clean up the house, and can even mix a mean martini. A few months after he built her, Trung brought her home to meet his parents at Christmas. She opened presents, and even participated in the family tradition of playing board games. It wasn't even that awkward, because she's programmed to speak 13,000 different sentences.

Aiko is spoken for, which means she's programmed to slap anyone (apart from Trung) who grabs or squeezes her. Trung also built sensors into her private parts, but claimed to reporters that he hasn't actually explored that part of their relationship yet.

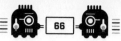

# MONKEY MACHINES

Young or old, rich or poor, we all have the same dream: to fly around in an Iron Man-like robotic suit and control it with our minds. That ultimate goal of human life is getting closer, as researchers at Duke University have built robotic exoskeletons that can be controlled by brains. There's only one problem—humans aren't the pilots; monkeys are.

Professor Miguel Nicolelis and his team of neuroscientists are busy creating brain-machine interfaces—implanting directly into gray matter electrodes that control robotic prostheses. The system allows users to move these mechanical arms and legs just by thinking. Researchers hope that one day such systems will help amputees and victims of paralysis. But for now, his team tests this technology exclusively on monkeys.

Using monkey test subjects makes sense, since Professor Nicolelis is understandably

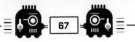

reluctant to implant experimental electrodes into a human's brain, nor would he be likely to find many willing test subjects. But that means these simian cyborgs now control robot arms, legs, and even full-sized human exoskeletons.

Since the electrodes operate wirelessly over a network, it's theoretically possible for one of these monkeys to manipulate its mecha machine half a world away. It's basically Curious George driving Voltron.

# ROBOT FIRSTS

**1927:** "Maria," a female robot, appears in Fritz Lang's science-fiction movie *Metropolis*. It's the first on-screen robot.

**1940:** Isaac Asimov publishes "Robbie" in *Super Science Stories*, the first piece of robot-themed fiction.

**1968:** "Humanoid Boogie" by the British group Bonzo Dog Doo-Dah Band is released, making it the first pop song about robots.

**1969:** A remote-controlled robot washes the windows of the Tower of the Americas in San Antonio, Texas.

**1983:** Ropet-HR, built by Personal Robotics Corporation, lobbies the House of Representatives for increased spending in robot technology. It is the first robot to address Congress.

**1983:** "Robot Redford" becomes the first robot to deliver a commencement address when it speaks to the graduating class at Anne Arundel Community College in Maryland.

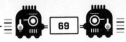

# EVIL ROBOT NAMESAKES

• iRobot is the name of the company that makes those adorable Roomba robotic vacuums. While that name may imply the company is following Apple's naming schism (iPhone, iPod, etc.), the company gets its name from *I, Robot*, the classic Isaac Asimov sci-fi novel about human-killing robots.

• Google's Chrome is the most popular web browser in the world. It's a source (and filter of) information for millions of people. Chrome is also the name of the robots that make up the totalitarian police force in George Lucas's 1971 film *THX 1138*.

• In his 1920 play *Rossum's Universal Robots*, Czech writer Karel Capek took *robota,* the Czech word for "forced labor" to coin "robot" to describe artificial men built to work in factories and serve as soldiers. They ultimately rise up and turn on humans. This is where we get the real-life word "robot."

# PLAY IT AGAIN, ROBOT

Robot musicians aren't uncommon. Chuck E. Cheese's (see pg. 167) has hosted millions of birthday parties, and the pioneering electronic band Kraftwerk replaces itself with robots during its live show, for example.

The tradition of automaton tunesmiths goes back to the mid-19th-century, when a music box could be programmed to play chimes from a rolling metal cylinder. By the 1840s, player pianos were able to play an actual musical instrument autonomously via scrolls with holes, a precursor to the punch-card computing of the 20th century.

The future of robotic music is a combination of these traditions: humanoid robots who actually play instruments.

• One such robot is Teotronica, which looks like the Terminator after its skin is burned off. Teotronica can sit at a piano and tickle the ivories with its cold machine hands. On its YouTube channel, the robot is shown playing everything from Mozart to R.E.M.

• The all-robot band Z-Machines, created by engineers at the University of Tokyo, features a guitar-playing robot with 78 fingers. (Beat that, Joe Satriani.)

It would be easy to dismiss these robots for merely recreating music and point out only humans can compose music, except of course that robots are already doing that, too. A computer program created at UC Santa Cruz, and given the creepily ordinary name "Emily Howell," was fed the work of classical composers and asked to recognize the patterns. Ms. Howell then created its own compositions, which classical music scholars rated as "excellent."

**—01000110—**

"Paro" is a robotic seal. It moves its head and flipper, makes seal noises, responds positively to touch and shuts down if it's struck. Paro's use? In animal therapy, a discipline in which patients are comforted by petting something soft and fuzzy.

# MCBLARE

In 2005 three members of Carnegie Mellon University's Robotics Institute wanted to do something to commemorate their program's 25th anniversary. They struck on the idea of doing something Scottish, in honor of the university's namesake, Scottish-American plutocrat and philanthropist Andrew Carnegie. There's nothing more Scottish than bagpipes, and so the trio created McBlare, the bagpiping 'bot ("Mc" to sound Scottish, "Blare" as in the sound of bagpipes).

McBlare consists of a set of bagpipes, which are played by a two-cylinder air compressor and electromagnets that power the fingers to open and close the holes that allegedly change the bagpipes' sound. McBlare is programmed with a library of 50 Scottish folk songs.

In 2006 McBlare—with its machinery covered in a tartan kilt in Carnegie Mellon's school colors—played at Piping Live, the International Piping Festival in Glasgow.

# AND HE WAS (A ROBOT)

David Byrne has had an eclectic career. In addition to his band, Talking Heads, he's written extensively, directed films, converted a church into a gigantic musical instrument, and one time even helped make a robot.

In his works, Byrne has often explored what it means to be human in an age of machines. As a result, the Museo Nacional Centro de Arte Reina Sofia in Madrid asked him to participate in a 2008 show called "Machines and Souls." He teamed with roboticist David Hanson, who uses a rubber-plastic material called "frubber" to create lifelike-looking humanoid robots that can also move and speak like humans because of tiny wires beneath their "flesh."

Together, Byrne and Hanson developed "Julio," a robot programmed with the voice of David Byrne, able to move its face and body in imitation of Byrne's signature bizarre facial expressions and herky-jerky dance movements.

# ROBOT ROCK

Daft Punk compose and perform music on electronic instruments and always wear metallic helmets. They may look like robots, but they're not Z-Machines, an electronic band that really is made up of robots.

Created by University of Tokyo engineer Kenjiro Matsuo, the band is a lightning-quick power trio of musical virtuosos, because they are programmed and built to be that way. The group consists of robot guitarist March, who has 78 fingers and wild rock-star hair made out of electrical cables; the 22-armed robot drummer Ashura; and on keyboards, Cosmo. Z-Machines' music is written by electronic-music composer Tom Jenkinson, who says that while the music does sound robotic, he thinks it's more akin to "'70s jazz fusion with a hint of prog."

Z-Machines played its first show in Tokyo in 2013 and released its debut album, the aptly titled *Music For Robots*, in 2014.

# JACKOTRON

We can all agree that Michael Jackson's masterpiece was *Captain EO,* the 3-D movie that played at Disneyland, featuring Jackson trying to bring music to a dystopian robot world. Clearly the man knew and enjoyed robots. So much so that at one point, Jackson had plans to become one.

In 2005, Jackson was in talks to star in a show at a Las Vegas casino. To promote it, a 50-foot-tall Michael Jackson robot would roam the Nevada desert, just beyond the Las Vegas airport. A robot that size would still be visible from the Las Vegas Strip, however, especially since it would shoot lasers from its eyes. It was even set to have had an expressive, moving face (unlike Jackson's real face).

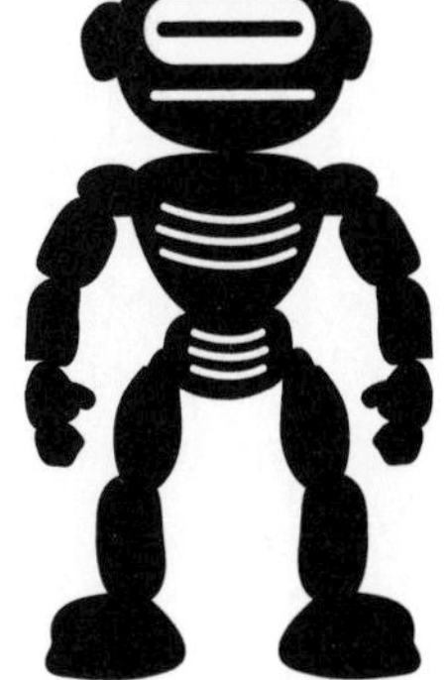

But Godzilla-sized robots are apparently prohibitively expensive, even for the King of Pop. The show, and the robot, were canceled entirely.

# WATCH THE SKIES

Aerial drones don't enjoy the best reputation. Militaries use them to remotely drop bombs, while governments use them to spy on nonviolent criminals. But not all drones are bad. Here are some good drones—if you don't cross them.

**Delivery drones.** In 2013, researchers at U.K.-based Aerosight teamed up with Domino's Pizza to develop pizza-delivery drones. Aerosight's "DomiCopter" successfully carried two pizzas to a customer a few miles from its launching point. Amazon.com has also announced plans to deliver packages with a fleet of drones called Amazon Prime Air. Despite these breakthroughs in human achievement and customer laziness, it might be a few years before these drones are in use—commercial drone flights aren't slated to be fully legalized in the U.S. until 2015.

**Sasquatch-searching drones.** Jeffrey Meldrum, an anthropology professor at Idaho State University, is in charge of "The Falcon Project," which aims to use a drone to look for Sasquatch. This proposed drone would utilize high-definition cameras and thermal-imaging equipment, in addition to a super-quiet motor, to sneak up on Bigfoot and capture video footage. As of press time, Meldrum and his team were still searching for enough funding to build it.

**Firefighting drones.** The MQ-1 UAV drone was used to fight massive California wildfires in 2013. Piloted by a member of the California National Guard from an airport hundreds of miles away, the MQ-1 UAV served as an "eye in the sky" for ground crews contending with the blaze. Unlike helicopters, which are difficult to operate at night and require refueling every few hours, these drones are lightweight and can stay in the air for up to 22 hours.

# YOU'RE MY INSPIRATION

**Bender (*Futurama*).** The hard-drinking, human-hating Bender was named for John Bender, the teen misanthrope portrayed by Judd Nelson in *The Breakfast Club,* one of co-creator Matt Groening's favorite movies.

**T-1000 (*Terminator 2: Judgment Day*).** The idea for the liquid metal robot that tries to assassinate Arnold Schwarzenegger's character came to writer-director James Cameron while he was eating a hot fudge sundae. He told his effects team that the robot had to look like a "spoon going into hot fudge; it dimples down, then flows up over and closes."

**Rosie (*The Jetsons*).** Voiced by Jean Vander Pyl, the Jetsons' robot maid was based on Shirley Booth's performance of a wisecracking maid on the 1960s sitcom *Hazel*. Hazel called her boss "Mr. B.," so Rosie called George Jetson "Mr. J."

**C-3PO and R2-D2 (*Star Wars*).** One of the inspirations for *Star Wars* is Akira Kurosawa's

1958 adventure movie, *Hidden Fortress*: It's about a strong-willed princess and her wise protector (sound familiar?). Comic relief is provided by a pair of bumbling farmers—directly related to C-3PO and R2-D2. As for the individual design and execution of the robots themselves:

• During a sound-mixing session on Lucas's previous film, *American Graffiti*, editor Walter Murch asked him for R2, D2 (Reel 2, Dialogue 2) of the film. Lucas liked the name so much that he made a note of it and eventually found the right character for it.

• C-3PO comes from Alex Raymond's science fiction novel *Iron Men of Mongo*. That book featured a copper-colored polite robot, who was shaped like a man and worked as a servant.

# PRESIDENT REBECCA

The 1984 presidential election couldn't have gone worse for the Democrats. After front-runners Ted Kennedy and Gary Hart dropped out, Walter Mondale was a sacrificial lamb against popular incumbent Ronald Reagan, who won in a 525-49 electoral vote beatdown. They should have nominated Rebecca.

In 1984 Dee and Sam Wright decided to start a family—a robot family. Rebecca, a feminine version of R2-D2 with Slinky hair, was the oldest of her four siblings. Described as an "overachiever" by her parents, Rebecca took an interest in politics and was entered into the New Hampshire and Washington Democratic primaries. She even had a 15-point platform called "High-Tech Leadership, Jobs, and Training" to promote what her parents saw was a lack of job training in preparing American workers for the 21st-century job market. Rebecca obviously didn't win—she received only three votes.

# SEXY ROBOTS FROM THE FUTURE

Along with the polling firm YouGov, the *Huffington Post* asked Americans about their attitudes toward robots. According to the responses, Joe Q. Public apparently expects mechanical maids: 58 percent said robots will soon be cleaning our homes, and 33 percent would take on a robot servant today. Since Roomba robotic vacuums are already the bane of cats everywhere, the *vox populi* might not be far off.

A near majority expect that robots will be driving cars and fighting in the military within 20 years. One in five predict that by 2030, robotic prostitutes will be all the rage. When asked "would you ever have sex with a robot?" 9 percent of respondents said "yes," while 11 percent said they "weren't sure." When asked if robot sex counted as cheating on a significant other, only 42 percent said "yes."

The people have spoken.

# HERON OF ALEXANDRIA

When one thinks of the ancient city of Alexandria, the Great Library and its famous destruction are probably what first come to mind. But Alexandria wasn't just home to some of the greatest scholars and their books. Thanks to the work of Heron of Alexandria, it was also the birthplace of modern robotics.

Heron was one of the greatest mathematicians of all time; if you recall your high school geometry, he developed Heron's Triangle and Formula. It was this prowess in mathematics that led to the engineering of many of today's modern conveniences. His most notable invention was the aeolipile, a primitive steam engine that predated the Industrial Revolution by nearly 2,000 years. He also created the world's first vending machine—a coin-operated holy water dispenser.

But Heron also deserves credit as one of the grandfathers of robotics. Inspired by Greek theater, Heron developed a ten-minute-long automated mechanical play that ran on strings, pulleys, and gears. So the next time you're watching the creepy singing robots at your local Chuck E. Cheese's, be sure to thank Heron of Alexandria for paving the way.

Some of the Grecian's other inventions include:

- **A wind-powered organ.** Heron created what is thought to be the first wind-powered machine in history after combining a windmill with the musical instrument. His attempt to attach a windmill to a tuba proved far less necessary.

- **The odometer.** In *On the Dioptra*, Heron described a two-wheeled cart that used falling pebbles within the machine to count the number of miles traveled.

***—01000110—***

**First American pop song about robots:** "Robot Man" by Connie Francis (1960). The narrator wants "a robot man to hold her tight," and it would be "impossible for him to speak."

# I'M POWERED UP FOR MY CLOSEUP

There's an old adage among actors in Hollywood: Never work with children or animals. Thanks to modern technology, they may soon have an alternative: working with robots.

A robot infant may be more efficient, as actors' unions allow babies to be on a set only a few hours a day or less, and even then their behavior is predictably unpredictable. That's why British special-effects artist Chris Clarke was recently hired by a soap opera (he won't say which one) to create an animatronic baby.

The robot baby perfectly mimics the herky-jerky, low-motor-control movement of a real baby, providing an effective time-saver for producers. Then, after filming the robot's scenes, a director can do what parents have been dreaming of since the dawn of time: turn it off.

# *TWILIGHT* COULD HAVE BEEN WORSE

The *Twilight* series of films has collectively grossed more than $3.3 billion. They were as critically panned as they were financially successful, with particular scorn placed on the wooden, expressionless acting of Kristen Stewart. But there was almost a real robot in the movies. And a baby one at that.

In *The Twilight Saga: Breaking Dawn—Part 2*, the character of human-vampire hybrid, rapidly-aging monster baby Renesmee was initially supposed to be played by a machine. At a cost of millions, the production company built a life-size robot baby for the role. But according to director Bill Condon, it was "one of the most grotesque things I've ever seen." It featured hollow, remote-controlled eyes and uncannily realistic rubber skin. The cast and crew nick-named it Chuckesmee, after the serial-killer doll Chucky from the *Child's Play* horror films.

Filmmakers went with a CGI baby instead.

# ROBOTS LIE!

Truth: The Georgia Institute of Technology set out to build robots that can lie. Researchers developed algorithms that allow this "lie-borg" to weigh the pros and cons of using deception. Two conditions must be met. First, there must be conflict between the robot and its opponent, say, a man vs. machine world war. Second, there must be a material benefit to the deception, like maybe creating a false reality to use our bodies as batteries. (Lying "just because"—the reason for most human dishonesty—wasn't included in programming.)

To test these algorithms, the Office of Naval Research funded a hide-and-seek experiment between a regular robot and a lying robot. By leaving deceptive clues, the lying robot was successfully able to evade the honest robot 75 percent of the time.

If you're disturbed by the idea of treacherous robots, you're not alone. The head of the project himself said, "We have been concerned with the ethical implications related to the creation of robots capable of deception."

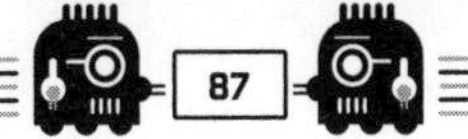


# PASSIVE-AGGRESSIVE ROBOT

Robots can be used for search-and-rescue missions or, not taking things that far, can help lost people. The Advanced Telecommunications Research Institute of Osaka, Japan, has created a friendly robot that monitors large groups of people and helps anyone it thinks might be lost. On a trial run at a local shopping mall, the robot gathered information from 16 cameras and several range finders to monitor 20 people and categorize their behavior. Among the criteria it looked for: walking fast, running, wandering, waiting, or simply looking "suspicious."

If it spots someone who looks "lost," the robot—about the size of a toddler—wheels up and asks if he or she needs assistance. If the robot is wrong and the person is just loitering, it recommends shops and restaurants.

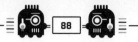

# BOT FOR TEACHER

At the beginning of each school year, every kid hopes for an easy year and a decent teacher, neither a mean old crone or an exhaustingly enthusiastic rookie. At Kudan Elementary School in Tokyo, kids may also be hoping they don't get Saya, the robot teacher.

Saya taught her first class to a group of ten-year-olds, educating them in science and technology, two subjects that are among her specialties. Although her skin gives off a plastic creepiness, she can exhibit a range of programmed movements designed to express six basic emotions: surprise, fear, disgust, anger, happiness, and sadness. She communicates through 18 motors that function as human muscles and enable her to smile, frown, and arch her eyebrows. She's also been programmed with 300 phrases and a 700-word vocabulary.

# THE EVOLUTION OF ASIMO

Honda is best known for its inexpensive cars, but since 1986, the company has also tinkered with robots. With the secretive "E Series" project, Honda has created an increasingly advanced group of robots. The first: E0, a bipedal robot capable of walking in a straight line. Getting down the human gait is a notoriously tough challenge for roboticists; E0 required a full five seconds between steps.

The E1 followed in 1987, which left E0 in the dust, able to trot at a blistering pace of 0.15 mph. By the time the project researched the E6 in 1993, Honda's robots could step over obstacles and slowly negotiate stairs.

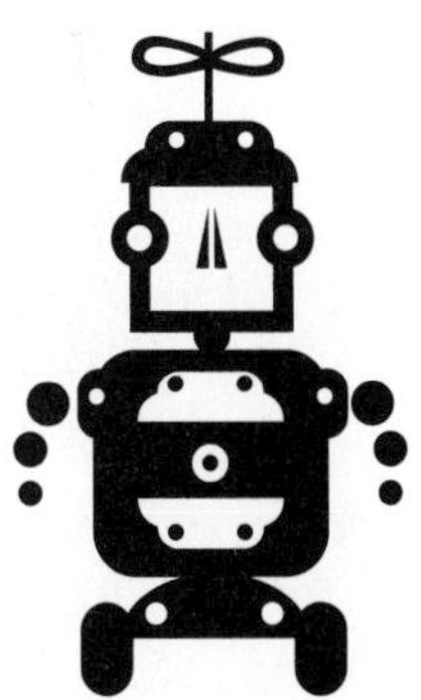

However, Honda kept it all secret. None of this progress in humanoid walking robots was revealed to the public until 1996, when it launched the P Series. This project culminated in the debut of the company's best-known bot to date: ASIMO, a high-tech automaton that has been rightfully called "the world's most advanced humanoid robot."

The original ASIMO, which debuted in October 2000, could walk at speeds of up to 1.8 mph. Unlike Honda's prior robots, it had a nifty new feature called "predicted movement control." This provided increased, more natural joint flexibility, and a more humanlike stride for the pint-sized robot, which resembles a kid in a spacesuit.

In the years that followed, ASIMO wowed audiences around the globe during public appearances at events like the annual Consumer Electronics Show in Las Vegas. Since 2005 ASIMO has also regaled crowds with a daily 15-minute demonstration at Innovations, an exhibit at Disneyland.

Honda rolled out the latest ASIMO in 2011. The current flagship robot is about the size of an elementary-school child, standing 4'3", and weighing 105 pounds. And it makes the once incredible E0 seem like a toy that a schoolchild would play with. The new ASIMO can run at speeds up to 5.6 mph. It uses two cameras mounted in its head to recognize faces and gestures. It can also shake hands, grasp objects, maneuver on uneven surfaces, recognize certain sounds, and even answer simple yes-or-no questions by nodding.

Honda hopes that with continued development, ASIMO will one day serve as an assistant to people with disabilities. It may also be able to venture into dangerous environments like forest fires and toxic spills, where humans fear to tread. But right now, ASIMO is a symbol of inspiration to robotics students and engineers around the world, a testament to this fascinating rapidly growing technology.

***—01000110—***

At a 2006 unveiling of a wine-identifying robot in Japan, press conference, a reporter and a cameraman put their hands in front of the robot's infrared beam. According to the robot, the reporter tasted like ham, and the cameraman tasted like bacon.

# THE PUKING ROBOT

"Larry," designed by microbiologist Catherine Makison at the U.K. Health and Safety Laboratory, is a watershed moment in robotics: It's the world's first fully operational vomiting robot.

It even has a legitimate, noble reason for existing. Makison's team created it to study the spread of the highly contagious *norovirus* on cruise ships, airplanes, and other densely populated spaces. Norovirus causes violent vomiting that persists for days, and Larry enables researchers to determine how far the virus travels and whether it becomes aerosolized.

After Larry pukes up a combination of water and luminescent fluid, scientists use a black light to check for traces of norovirus in the air and a grid on the floor that measures distance traveled. Researchers hope that the data gathered can lead to better understanding of norovirus and prevent isolated instances from becoming massive outbreaks.

# GEE YOUR HAIR SMELLS LIKE ROBOTS!

Japan has a sizable elderly population, and an equally sizable portion of the robotics industry is devoted to making robots to serve them. Panasonic's newest entry in the robots-for-the-old world: Head Care Robot. It can wash and style old people's hair, two things that can fall by the wayside in overstaffed assisted living facilities.

Head Care Robot uses a series of sensors to three-dimensionally scan the head and determine the amount of pressure needed to clean and massage each particular scalp. Then 24 mechanical fingers and a series of warm-water nozzles go to work: eight fingers massage the back of the neck; the rest knead the scalp and apply shampoo and conditioner. Once the robot rinses the product fully out of the hair, warm air blow-dries it completely.

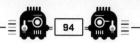

# BOT THOUGHTS

"The robot is going to lose. Not by much. But when the final score is tallied, flesh and blood is going to beat the damn monster."

**—Adam Smith**

"Robots do not hold on to life. They can't. They have nothing to hold on with—no soul, no instinct. Grass has more will to live than they do."

**—Karel Capek**

"Unless mankind redesigns itself by changing our DNA through altering our genetic makeup, computer-generated robots will take over our world."

**—Stephen Hawking**

"I visualize a time when we will be to robots what dogs are to humans. I'm rooting for the machines."

**—Claude Shannon**

# SOFT LAUNCH

Robots of the future must be versatile to perform all the tasks we expect of them, but according to the Laboratory of Intelligent Systems in France, they have to be physically versatile, too—as in soft, squishy, malleable, and even modular.

That's why LIF is on the forefront of the "soft robotics" movement. Honestly, they look like water-filled plastic baggies or transparent jellyfish. Through a process called *electroadhesion*, these robot parts can organize and attach to each other to create larger robots.

The surfaces of each are charged with different voltage levels. That creates an attraction between two soft robots, which then connect their squishy selves to each other. This is a small but key development in robots. Once the modular process is perfected, things like shape-shifting instructions can be programmed, and surface sensors can be placed, making these robots' abilities wildly varied.

# SMELL-BOTS

The Tohoku Earthquake of 2011 was the largest in Japanese history. But life's worst often brings out humanity's best, and this earthquake inspired one man to help the world… by building a robot dog to detect stinky feet.

Shuntaro-kun is a life-sized dogbot with built-in odor sensors and custom hardware to specifically analyze foot-stink. If your feet smell great, Shuntaro-kun will lovingly cuddle up to you. If they smell terrible, he'll growl threateningly. And if your feet are among the worst in his database, it will roll over and play dead.

Conceived by the president of toymaker CrazyLabo, Shuntaro-kun was meant to make people laugh during tough times. But if you think he's closer to creepy than cute, wait until you meet his master. Kaori-chan is another olfactory-oriented automaton designed by CrazyLabo: She's the disembodied head of a female robot designed to smell (and insult) your bad breath. A typical reaction: "Yuck! I can't stand it!" Her worst? "There's an emergency! That's beyond the limit of patience!"

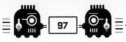

# ROBOT MUSCLES

Even when a robot looks human, under the hood it's usually anything but. Hydraulics, pulleys, and other mechanical systems are rigged to mimic human movement. But one researcher has made a breakthrough that could finally allow robots to get totally cut and walk around with their shirts off: robotic muscles.

Dr. Adrien Koh of the University of Singapore has created an artificial muscle made of polymer that responds to electrical impulses in the same way as actual human tissue. The polymer muscles expand and contract, and are capable of lifting 10 times their own weight. This would make a robot powered by its own muscles far stronger—and more energy efficient—than one powered by mechanical systems.

The polymer muscles also convert mechanical energy to electrical energy, meaning after an initial charge, they could be self-powered.

# SHAKE YOUR ROBO-BOOTY

Does the world really need a robotic butt? Maybe not, but, in 2012 Japanese engineer Nobuhiro Takahashi and his colleagues at the University of Electro-Communications in Chofu decided to build one anyway. What did he call his incredibly odd invention? SHIRI, which is a fairly crude Japanese slang term for "buttocks."

Takahashi's animatronic bum-bum consists of a waist, thighs, and a pair of alarmingly authentic-looking butt cheeks. SHIRI definitely resembles the real deal but underneath its outer layer of silicon skin and foam, there's a complex series of wires and a metallic skeleton.

SHIRI might make an excellent training tool for, on one end, proctology students or, on the other, unethical massage therapists. But instead of all that, Takahashi says he was most interested in studying how the butt reacts to stimuli, emotionally speaking. His team added a "gluteus maximus actuator," which are robotic muscles that inflate or deflate SHIRI in order to convey its mood. When the butt is in a good mood, it happily pulsates. When it's frightened, it twitches like a frightened squirrel.

These moods are activated by the actions of the user, which SHIRI tracks via a microphone embedded in its skin. The butt can "feel" slaps, pokes, strokes, and touches.

***—01000110—***

Australian medical technology company Enterix has built a robot named Grace that can detect bowel cancer at a 98% accuracy rate. It analyzes tissue samples in five seconds, reducing the need for invasive colonoscopies. Enterix estimates that if Grace were run 24 hours a day, Australia's entire population could be screened for bowel cancer in just one year.

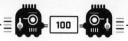

# THE EXOSKELETON KEY

Over the last five years there has been an explosion in the design of exoskeletons that make average human beings capable of extraordinary feats. For example, after the 2011 Fukushima nuclear disaster in Japan, Cyberdyne's Hal-5 enabled rescue personnel to safely traverse areas that would otherwise have been too toxic or treacherous to search for survivors.

Claire Lomus was a marathon runner who had become paralyzed from the chest down after an accident. She never thought she'd compete, let alone walk, again until she heard about Argo's ReWalk exoskeleton. That model is the first robotic suit to interpret the faint electrical signals that still fire in damaged muscles (that have nowhere to travel because of paralysis), and use them to manipulate the suit's motorized joint. In 2011 Lomus became the first person to run a marathon with an exoskeleton.

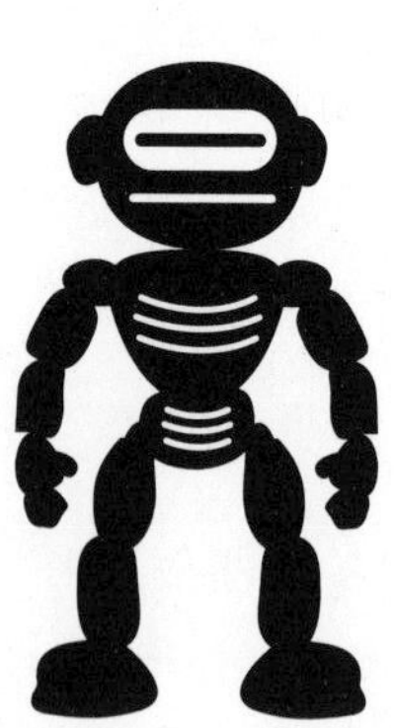

# HULC SMASH

Despite centuries of military innovations, the backbone of any army has remained the lowly grunts. You can train them and you can strengthen them with push-ups, but the limitations of the human body still put an upper cap on what they can do. Until now.

The Human Universal Load Carrier, which just so happens to create the awesome acronym HULC, is a robotic exoskeleton that can be worn by the common soldier. The hydraulic-powered frame allows soldiers to carry more gear and could be tricked out with various sensors and other technology to enhance the fighting prowess of Joe Infantryman.

Work on the HULC system began in 2000 at Berkeley Robotics, and in 2009 it was licensed to Lockheed Martin. It is currently undergoing field tests and might soon be field deployed by the U.S. Army.

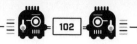

# MAN SLINKY

Futurists have long made promises that scientists couldn't keep: moon bases, food pills, and a cure for the common cold, for example. More importantly, where are our robotic exoskeletons? They're here!

Meet the Spring-Walker Exoskeleton. A surprisingly low-tech but devilishly innovative system, the Spring-Walker is a back-mounted device that allows the user to "fly." By directing the kinetic energy stored in high-tension springs, Spring-Walkers can jump many times farther than our dumb meat legs will allow. A large enough Spring-Walker could allow the wearer to literally leap tall buildings in a single bound.

Is it basically a robot pogo stick? Yes. But does it look like that sweet suit Ripley used in *Aliens*? Also yes.

# INTERNET FOR ROBOTS

When you need an answer fast, what do you do? You get on the Internet. But what do robots do when they haven't been programmed with the information they need to complete a task? They get on the Internet, too—the robots-only Internet.

In 2009 researchers at five European robotics labs created a mini-Internet, for robots only, called RoboEarth. It uses a cloud-based storage system called Rapyuta (named after a robot-occupied castle in the animated film *Castle in the Sky*) to store data and information uploaded by all five labs, which robots can then share with one another.

Every situation and task that robots hooked up to RoboEarth have ever done is cataloged on Rapyuta, which can then be downloaded or "learned" by other robots instantly. One example: a hospital-based robot could send its floor-plan map to a floor-cleaning robot assigned to clean that same hospital.

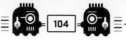

# SLUGBOT

While slugs themselves are slow, they can destroy crops at an alarmingly quick pace—as many as 200 of the little buggers can be found in a square meter of wheat.

British inventor Ian Kelly devised the SlugBot hoping to eliminate the need for harsh pesticides and save farmers millions in lost revenue. SlugBot is the size of a lawn mower, with multi-terrain wheels and a long arm attached to its front. The end of the arm shines a red LED light onto the ground, which allows cameras to record and send information to a computer that identifies slugs. When SlugBot hits the jackpot, it uses an additional mechanical arm to grasp, lift, and drop the slug into a hopper. Bacteria inside of the robot consume the slug and convert the released energy into electrons that can be utilized to fuel the battery.

In other words, SlugBot fuels its quest to eat slugs...by eating slugs.

# ROACH-BOTS

Roaches are social insects who just can't resist a crowd. This is probably why you never find one under your sink—you find 20.

Scientists at the Free University of Brussels tried to manipulate this communal instinct by building tiny roach-bots. These bionic bugs, covered in authentic roach pheromones, were then sent in to peer-pressure their biological brothers. In over 60 percent of trials, the real roaches followed the robot roaches to hiding spots.

What are the practical applications for this research? It's possible similar *doppelgänger* devices might someday help with pest control. But the experiment has been most valuable as a proof of concept, suggesting a similar strategy might work with other animals—which is the only valid reason for putting more cockroaches into the world.

# GISMO THE PEACEFUL

"Gismo the Peaceful," created by 14-year-old Woody Fuehrer in 1954, harkens back to the aw-schucks, gee-whiz heyday of the Boy Scouts, when robotics represented a new pastime for all-American children bored with making phones out of tin cans and string.

Resembling a scrawny Tin Man of Oz, Gismo stood nearly six feet tall on lanky legs fashioned from painted two-by-fours, which supported a pretzel-can body and oil-drum head. There is no clear reason why Gismo needed to be nearly six feet tall and almost 100 pounds, as his primary function was to serve cookies with his arms and rudimentary hands, though gradual improvements enabled him to light up, buzz a buzzer, and play records.

Fuehrer began exhibiting Gismo in his hometown of Cranston, Rhode Island, and quickly racked up public accolades, grants from scientific bodies, and even an endorsement offer from the U.S. Pretzel Institute. At the height of his popularity, Gismo made appearances on NBC's *Today*, where he nearly got into a fistfight with the show's then-cohost J. Fred Muggs, a chimpanzee.

Gismo truly found his place in the cultural zeitgeist in an article in *Boys' Life* magazine in 1956. The article included basic plans for readers to create their own version of Gismo at home, which surely spawned a small army of Gismos across the United States, although probably many more half-finished, motionless heaps of pretzel cans in garages.

In the decades that followed, *Boys' Life* regularly published plans for updated versions of Gismo, with the latest, Gismo 5, appearing as recently as 2011. Sadly, the plans for Gismo's later iterations devolved into little more than plastic buckets and accessories mounted on remote-controlled toy cars. Even with an environmentally-friendly emphasis on recycling used plastic, these Gismos lack the can-do charm of their predecessor, a testament to the value of elbow grease and teenage ingenuity.

# RATS

Engineers have long tried to build small robots that can navigate through rubble to find disaster victims, without much success. Meanwhile, rats have shown that they have the brains and agility to perform search missions—but only in a laboratory setting. Let them outside the lab, and the rats do pretty much whatever they want.

So physiologists at the University of New York have combined the best of both worlds to create RoboRat, a cyborg (part animal, part machine) rodent that will go anywhere it's told. A tiny backpack carries a miniature video camera; tiny electrodes go into its brain. A human controller can guide RoboRat with a laptop computer, sending signals directly to the pleasure center of the rat's brain, rewarding the animal if it does what it's told.

The scientists are surprised how easily this is done—they've even been able to get the robots to climb trees, something most rats don't do.

# TURTLE SOUP

Beginning in the 1930s, William Grey Walter made huge discoveries about the brain with EEG technology. (He figured out how to use delta waves to find brain tumors and discovered the lesions that cause epilepsy, for example.) And in 1948, Walter designed the first robots that could make "decisions" on their own.

To demonstrate his thesis—that a relatively few brain cells could control complex behaviors—Walter made an artificial representation. He called his two simple palm-sized robots the Machina Speculatrix ("speculative machines") as a whole, but "Elmer" and "Elsie" individually. Walter nicknamed them "turtles," since they were shaped like turtles and moved slowly.

With very little computing power onboard (it was 1948, after all), Walter programmed the robots to ride around on their three wheels, and, when sensing a low battery, to return to a charging station. That's called *phototaxis*, and it represents the first instance robotic autonomy, a landmark scientific moment.

# THE PRAYING ROBOT

One would think that the connection between robots and a higher, divine power would be confined to the shrieked lament of "Save us, God, from the robots!" during some kind of future robot uprising.

Not so. An Iranian schoolteacher named Akbar Rezaie has built a robot that teaches and encourages kids to pray. After witnessing a relative become entranced by a dancing doll, Rezaie wondered how he could use children's natural enjoyment of robots for something more productive, such as the daily prayers dictated by his Shiite Muslim faith. So he ordered a robot kit from a South Korean company, modified it to make prayer movements, and programmed it with the voice of a Quran chanter (the Western, Christian equivalent is a lector) to say prayer phrases and prompts.

He named it Veldan, a phrase that translates to "Youth of Heaven."

# SAN DIEGO BOT-RE

In 1562, Don Carlos, heir to the throne of Spain, fell down a flight of stairs and nearly died. King Philip II couldn't bear the thought of his son's death, so he did what any concerned father would do—he dug up the corpse of a dead monk, Diego de Alcala, and dropped the body into bed with his son. Philip then bargained with God: Allow Diego to save his son, and he'll honor the Lord. The next morning, Don Carlos was okay...minus the dead monk in his bed.

To repay God, King Philip II commissioned a clockmaker to construct a wind-up automaton in the image of Diego. The creation stood 15 inches tall—a remarkable replica of the human form, especially for work done 450 years ago. The automaton can walk, turn and bow its head, raise a cross, and open and close its mouth. It's currently stored at the Smithsonian. (The real Diego was returned to his grave.)

# FATHER ROBOT

Should the Catholic church ever find itself in an irreversible priest shortage, there are always robots. The Last Moment Robot, designed by artist Dan Chen, is little more than a smooth white robotic "arm" that can effectively give its own form of "last rites." It grasps the hand of a dying human, while a nearby speaker emits a synthetic voice speaking words of "comfort."

"I am sorry that your family and friends can't be with you right now, but don't be afraid," the android says. "I am here to comfort you. You are not alone; you are with me. Your family and friends love you very much; they will remember you after you are gone."

The Last Moment Robot is less a prototype and more of a provocative statement on technology and humanity. Chen utilized his creation as part of his master's thesis at Rhode Island's School of Design, entitled "File > Save As > Intimacy."

# ANGELIC AUTOMATONS

Seems like every time you open the newspaper (on your web browser), all you find is lying, cheating, and worse. For while humanity's getting crueler all the time, the opposite may be happening with robots.

Researchers in Switzerland set out to test a theory about the biological roots of altruism. They built inch-long robots on wheels programmed to forage for tiny silicon "food" discs. After each round, the robots with the least food were "deleted"—their programming was replaced by a mix of programming from the more successful robots.

Repeating this process over and over created a sort of robot evolution, where the most successful foraging strategies were passed on, and the worst died out. And guess what? Those Darwinian robots got friendlier. Robots with similar programming—families, essentially—began sharing more and more food as their selfish competitors died out.

# DARPA GRAND CHALLENGE

What do voice-to-text software, GPS, and the Internet all have in common? Each of them began as a top-secret Pentagon research project funded by DARPA, the Defense Advanced Research Projects Agency, the futuristic research arm of the U.S. Department of Defense.

In 2002, the Pentagon announced plans to convert a third of its battlefield vehicles into autonomous intelligent machines by 2015. Instead of keeping its plans secret, the Pentagon tapped into the brainpower of the civilian robotics industry by sponsoring the 2004 DARPA Grand Challenge, a robots-only off-road race through the Mojave Desert.

The challenge: to build a robot programmed to navigate a 142-mile course in under ten hours, through unpredictable terrain with zero human assistance. The teams, mostly university researchers sponsored by private firms, had two years to build their machines before the March 2004 race. The prize: $1 million and the possibility of some government contracts.

The result? An embarrassment. Ghostrider,

the only motorcycle in the race, fell down at the starting line and didn't get up. A truck couldn't navigate a foot-long rock, and a bath-tub-shaped robot flipped over on the first turn. After veering off course or getting stuck on hills, half of the cars broke down in the first mile.

While none of the robots came close to finishing, the best performance came from Carnegie Mellon University's Sandstorm, a robotic Humvee built by the Red Team, led by Professor "Red" Whittaker. (The robot? It was red.) Sandstorm made it seven miles before it went the wrong way in a turn and got stuck straddling a berm, unable to move. Then its wheels caught fire. Nevertheless, the next day, DARPA announced the 2005 Grand Challenge.

Eighteen months later, 43 teams met at the California Speedway to qualify for the race that netted a $2 million purse. The robots had learned a lot in a year and a half. Sandstorm was back, and with it came Highlander, an identical red Humvee also from the Red Team. Both qualified for the big race.

Another finalist, newcomer Stanley, a blue Volkswagen from Stanford University, was the

only robot who didn't hit a single obstacle in pre-trials. Stanley's strategy was different; while all of the other robots used lasers to scan the terrain just ahead of them, Stanley combined that ability with data from a video camera that let it see farther up ahead to the horizon. That enabled it to drive up to 40 mph over terrain that it had never seen before.

The 2005 DARPA Grand Challenge saw 23 robots qualify to race on a new 132-mile course through the Mojave Desert. When all but one made it past the 7.4-mile mark, the teams settled in to watch video from the DARPA chase vehicles.

Highlander took the lead in the first 30 miles, with Stanley and Sandstorm just a few minutes behind. The field of 22 dwindled as robot cars failed to navigate tight turns or climb steep hills. Some lost direction when their laser rangefinders were knocked off. By mile 50, only seven cars were left. With 30 miles to go,

Stanley passed Highlander, who was having trouble reaching higher speeds. Sandstorm was making up ground on both of them, but it wasn't enough to win. After six hours and 53 minutes, Stanley became the first self-driving robot to complete a 132-mile desert road race, with an average speed of 19 mph.

DARPA called the Grand Challenges "the dawn of the self-driving car revolution," and to date the military operates more than 12,000 driverless vehicles. They've replicated that success with other Challenges. When the 2007 Urban Challenge brought robot driving technology to the city streets, Stanford's Junior came in second. At the 2015 DARPA Robotics Challenge, automated machines will perform cleanup and rescue missions after (simulated) natural or man-made disasters.

***—01000110—***

In 2010, roboticists in Japan built a robot penguin. Why? To see if real penguins would follow a robot penguin. They did, forming a line behind the robot as it led them to a pool. (It also "smokes" a pipe for some reason.)

# ROBOT, CHICKEN

Human beings have been evolving for millennia, and we can now do amazing things, like make cheese sandwiches and post pictures of cheese sandwiches on Instagram. What we can't do: debone 1,500 chickens in an hour.

To correct this evolutionary anomaly, the Japanese company Mayekawa has invented a robot that can rapidly tear the meat off a chicken carcass.

The automatic deboner first analyzes each chicken's size and shape so that it can precisely remove as much meat as possible from the bone, eliminating waste and increasing the amount of delicious chicken meat you get to shove down your gullet. Unfortunately, the deboner looks less like a typical robot and more like an eight-foot-tall nightmare of pneumatic tubes, infrared cameras, and (obviously) spinning blades.

# FLEXPICKER

In a perfect world, we would all eat fresh food, not boxed junk. But in our decent world, that processed junk could get into the box with the help of a cool robot.

The IRB 360, also known by the much friendlier FlexPicker, is an industrial robot used in food-sorting and packaging facilities. FlexPicker looks like a cross between a slow cooker and a daddy long legs. It has a large white "base box" with several long, jointed arms that can grab items off a conveyor belt and stack or sort them into neat piles, which can then be packaged and sold to people who don't worry too much about where their food comes from.

FlexPicker can pick and sort just about anything that needs picking and sorting, including pancakes, candy, frozen pizzas, and snack-sized salami slices. In an enjoyable and informative video on the manufacturer's website, we see a squadron of FlexPickers tirelessly sorting little salamis into rows so they can be boxed up, shipped out, and subsequently purchased by you at a gas station.

# SO PROSTHETIC

• Bertolt Meyer, a psychologist at the University of Zurich, has spent his entire life wearing a prosthetic left hand. In his teens he had a movable hook rigged to a pulley system that he operated by flexing his shoulders. Embarrassed, Meyer hid his disability under gloves and long sleeves. Now in his 30s, he's proud to be one of the first to wear the i-Limb, a $100,000 bionic hand complete with individual finger control, a rotatable wrist, and a skin-colored cover. The i-Limb has 24 grip patterns, and he can manipulate the appendage through an app on his iPhone.

• Two-year-old Zaxton Waters, from Leander, Texas, was born without three fingers on his left hand. His older brother Christian decided to get him a new hand. Christian found an adult-sized prosthetic and brought it to his old high school, hoping to use the school's 3-D printer to make a smaller version. Instead, teacher Herb Wasson enlisted three of his students, and the group worked after hours—and without extra credit—to build one themselves. The team successfully gave Zaxton a prosthetic hand that

he can open and close by bending his wrist, letting him pick up things that he couldn't before.

• Jason Barnes lost his right arm in an industrial accident in 2012, but he didn't let that end his dream of being a professional drummer. After transforming an arm brace and springs into an over-the-shoulder harness, Jason re-learned how to play and enrolled in the Atlanta Institute of Music. There he met roboticist Gil Weinberg, who specializes in robots that can listen and interact with human musicians. In 2014 Weinberg built a prosthetic arm that Barnes can control with electrical impulses from his bicep. The device holds one drumstick that responds to Barnes' arm movements and a second drumstick fitted with a microphone that picks up the beat. The second drumstick plays along all by itself. "We were able to create some surprises," Weinberg said, "with music that cannot be created by humans alone."

# RING IT UP, ROBOT

While trying to create a grocery-bagging robot, a team at Stanford was faced with a problem. When a robot wants to grab an unknown item, normally it needs its grip to be correctly programmed by a human. But in the case of a supermarket checkout line, there's no time to program each individual item. So the Stanford Personal Robotics Crew figured out that as long as each item has a similar shape to the robot's hand-grip, it was able to bag with a high rate of success. The resulting PR2 robot also comes with a built-in scanner that reads each item's UPC code before bagging the item.

Okay, it's more of a "tossing the item indiscriminately into a grocery bag." It's not perfect, but at least you don't have to make small talk with a 15-year-old.

# RACK 'EM UP, ROBOT

Getting hustled by a pool shark is a bad way to spend a night, especially when you thought his low-key demeanor made *him* the sucker. But when you get hustled by a 500-pound robot, you really have nobody to blame but yourself.

Thomas Nierhoff, a graduate student at the Institute of Automatic Control Engineering at the Technical University of Munchen, created a pool-playing robot. The humanoid is built with two anthropomorphic arms that can firmly shoot a pool stick, which it monitors with the built-in camera in its head. That "head" syncs with a ceiling-mounted camera to send data back to the robot about shot accuracy and optimal shooting variations.

Nierhoff ran more than 400 test strokes and found that his robot was able to make up to 80 percent of his shots from easier angles. Just like a human, the robot had more trouble with those trick shots, the ones that require a graduate degree in geometry.

# QUAKEBOT

On March 17, 2014, *Los Angeles Times* writer Ken Schwencke (and thousands of other Californians) were awakened by an earthquake. Schwencke broke the story online less than three minutes after the 4.7-magnitude quake struck.

The real "writer" of the post wasn't really Schwencke. It was an algorithm, a robot, he created called Quakebot. Schwencke set it up so that when the U.S. Geological Survey detects an earthquake over a certain size, Quakebot extracts certain data from the USGS report—time, location, severity—and uses it to fill in the blanks on an "earthquake report" template. A human editor then reads it and posts it.

The end result reads just like a sedate, hard-news brief: "A shallow magnitude 4.7 earthquake was reported Monday morning five miles from Westwood, California, according to the U.S. Geological Survey." Of all the robots in this book, this one might be the most terrifying—hey, we're writers, and we like our jobs.

# THE WONDERFUL WORLD OF DISNEY ROBOTS

"Disneyland will never be completed. It will continue to grow as long as there is imagination left in the world," Walt Disney said about his first theme park shortly after its opening in 1955. Disney was constantly looking for ways to enhance his labor of love, and that often involved robots.

The park already featured simple animated figures that operated on hydraulics in the Jungle Cruise, but Walt was looking for something much more exciting. Inspired by a mechanical bird he'd acquired, Disney asked "Imagineers" Roger Broggie and Wathel Rogers to add some additional features to turn the bird into "Little Man," a mechanical man that could "dance" like actor Buddy

Ebsen. (Bosses are weird.) It was a great start, but the robot required an immense amount of mechanics that wouldn't have been practical as a Disneyland attraction. Another problem was that Little Man was only nine inches tall.

The duo and their robotics team continued to tinker in what Disney coined "Audio-Animatronics," and in 1963 Disneyland opened the Enchanted Tiki Room. The attraction was filled with more than 150 singing and dancing mechanical birds, animals, statues, and flowers. This was nothing compared to the company's next phase in robotics.

At the 1964 World's Fair in New York City, the company rolled out a robotic Abraham Lincoln for the State of Illinois pavilion. The robot was able to rise from a chair, move his arms, and deliver excerpts from several of the beloved president's speeches. More Disney bots entertained attendees in the Carousel of Progress, later moved to Disneyland. The exhibits included robotic dinosaurs and dozens of singing dolls from a Disneyland attraction called It's a Small World (and now the song is stuck in your head).

Coasting on rave reviews from the Fair, Imagineers got to work on even more fantastical attractions featuring Audio-Animatronics. Within a few years, dozens of rambunctious (and robotic) buccaneers could be found singing “”Yo Ho (A Pirate’s Life for Me)” in the Pirates of the Caribbean. In 1969, a small army of animatronic “grim grinning ghosts” moved into the Haunted Mansion next door.

Disney’s bots have grown increasingly sophisticated. An animatronic Stitch (from *Lilo & Stitch*) in the Stitch’s Great Escape ride can move its entire body. The Magic Kingdom’s Hall of Presidents has a complete set of 43 robot presidents. And Dr. Bunsen Honeydew and Beaker of the Muppets star in Muppet Mobile Lab. These “living character” robots freely roam parks and interact with guests, remotely controlled by puppeteers. In 2009, a team of Imagineers created Otto, which can hear, see, hold conversations, and understand when someone is happy.

# ROBOCUP

What's one of the most consistently innovative and quickly developing fields of robotics? Robot soccer.

The Robot Soccer World Cup (or "RoboCup") is exactly what it sounds like. The tournament has grown from 38 teams in the first year (1997) to more than 500, with participants from all around the world. Organizers have set a lofty goal for the competition: By 2050, they want a robot team to defeat the winners of the World Cup of human soccer (probably Brazil).

As of today…the robots still have a long way to go. Matching the human gait is such a challenge, the humanoid robots amble and knock the ball more rather than run and take power kicks. But there is still hope that designers will soon be able to teach the robots more advanced soccer techniques, such as diving and begging the ref to call a penalty.

# SWEEPING THE NATION

Sure, the Massachusetts Institute of Technology once won a national championship in tiddlywinks (really), but it's MIT's academics that make it world famous. However, that doesn't mean that they don't love competition.

Sweeping the Nation is an annual robotics competition at MIT that challenges engineering students to build a utilitarian and creative trash-picking robot. Students are given an identical kit of components but then must use their imaginations to create the best bot possible. Once the robots are built, the machines are set to task picking up soda cans. Extra points are given to robots that can crush the soda cans before depositing them in designated "goals" or to those that steal trash from their opponent's side of the field. Robots that advance past the preliminary rounds then face off against each other in a single-elimination round. And what do the winners of Sweeping the Nation receive? A free T-shirt!

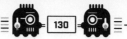

# HELLO, NURSE

Hospitalized Japanese patients and elderly persons residing in assisted-living facilities can look forward to less human interaction than ever before, now that Riba the robotic nurse is making its way into the mainstream.

Developed by researchers at RIKEN and Tokai Rubber Industries, Riba was created to address the growing population of elderly and ill individuals who require physical assistance. However, Riba looks like a blue polar bear and can and will lift patients. Riba is outfitted with rubber tactile sensors on the arms and chest that provide guidance enabling it to move patients from their beds to wheelchairs, the bathroom, and other necessities. Riba is the first interactive "body assistant" that will be used in mainstream medical and long-term-care facilities. If nothing else, Riba is certainly an interesting way to break the monotony of nursing home life.

# SICK ROBOT

The biggest drawback for medical students studying cadavers is that they can't say what was wrong with them—the student has to find out. And while young doctors learn how to diagnose and treat live patients at teaching hospitals, you can't teach medical students how to cure a certain illness on a certain day without poisoning the local water supply the night before the big lesson on bacteria.

Researchers at the Gifu University's Graduate School of Medicine in Japan created a robotic "sick patient" that can mimic the symptoms and movements of a human patient suffering through whatever disease or injury that the poor robot has been programmed to endure. The robot can even tell medical professionals exactly where it is feeling pain...by talking. This robotic innovation allows veteran physicians to teach their students how to treat specific injuries without hoping that someone comes in with a broken neck on the day you scheduled "how to treat broken necks."

# A NOT-SO-HARD DRIVE

Driving is such a hassle. You have to keep your hands on the wheel, remember where you're going, and pay attention. Who has the time?

Google is self-driving cars at its headquarters in Mountain View, California. The Google robotic car is a Toyota Prius outfitted with $150,000 of upgrades, including a laser that maps the car's immediate environment. While the cars have caused no reported accidents and follow all traffic laws, one resident complained they are a safety hazard—drivers may be so spooked by driverless cars that they're more likely to crash themselves.

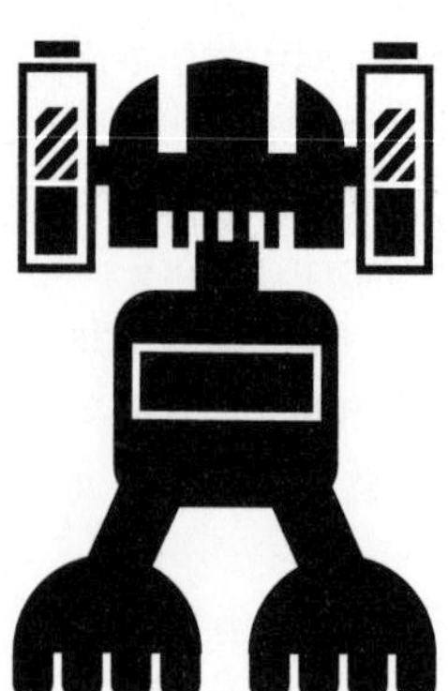

Experts say that fully autonomous cars may hit the market in as little as five years. The biggest roadblock: Four states actually have laws banning autonomous vehicles.

# ROBO VAN

In 1995 scientists at Carnegie Mellon's robotics department created NavLab5: an otherwise normal 1990 Pontiac TransSport minivan outfitted with a number of robotic components. A video camera mounted near the rearview mirror would survey the road for lane markings, ruts, and curbs, and send the information to a computer stuck between the van's front seats. The computer, in turn, would send instructions on how to steer to the electric motor controlling the steering wheel.

Here's the extra-remarkable part: creators Dean Pomerleau and Todd Jochem rode along in the van as it drove itself 3,000 miles across the country from Pittsburgh to Los Angeles. NavLab5 did 98 percent of the steering; all Pomerleau and Jochem did on the "No Hands Across America Tour" was operate the throttle and brake, and fill up the gas tank.

# NO VOLKS IN THE WAGEN

"Volkswagen" loosely translates to "people's wagon," but who needs people when you've got robots?

The German auto engineers are in development on a program called Temporary Auto Pilot. It allows the car to drive itself, at least for a while, at speeds of up to 80 mph with the use of cameras, radar, and ultrasonic sensors. The system can read speed limit and other traffic signs, and adaptive cruise control can modulate speed using radar to sense the presence of a slower car ahead. A lane-departure-warning system and a lane-keep-assistance system even keeps cars inside their lane at all times.

Volkswagen says that robotic cars will actually make traffic go faster, since it will eliminate silly human driver quirks, like rubbernecking and unnecessary panic stops.

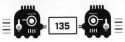

# ROBOT LAWN MOWERS

In our long quest for better living (okay, laziness) through robots, few devices have inspired more innovation than the lawn mower—it's a pain to mow the lawn. Since the 1950s, dozens of robotic lawn mowers have been produced, patented, and theorized.

Early models were not fully automated, but remote-controlled. Queen Elizabeth II tried out such a mower at the 1959 Chelsea Flower Show. By 1961 *Radio Electronics* featured a fully automated mower, which followed a set path over buried radio wire. Around the same time, an electronics trade group proposed a mower that would respond to voice commands (which is no different than just making your kids mow).

Today, several robotic lawn mowers are on the market, including one by the makers of the Roomba vacuum cleaner. Most require a buried wire to denote the perimeter of the cutting area and then return themselves to a docking/charging station when complete. They don't even want a beer when they're done.

# SERPEX

On May 1, 2009, the *Spirit* Mars rover suffered a catastrophic setback, an interplanetary disaster that ended the mission and the brave rover's robot life. What happened? It got stuck in the sand. You don't need to be a rocket scientist to know that losing a $400 million robot in the rough, millions of miles away, is a bummer. Which is why engineers are now building synthetic space snakes, of course.

The Serpentine Robots for Planetary Exploration project, ominously abbreviated to SERPEX, is tasked with designing snakelike robotic astronauts. By slithering, burrowing, and undulating through the Martian landscape, these cyborg serpents will be able to navigate hard-to-reach nooks and crannies with a reduced risk of getting stuck like *Spirit*. The plan is to eventually include one or more such viper droids as detachable appendages on a future Mars rover.

A remote-controlled roverbot would essentially have a remote-controlled snakebot. If we

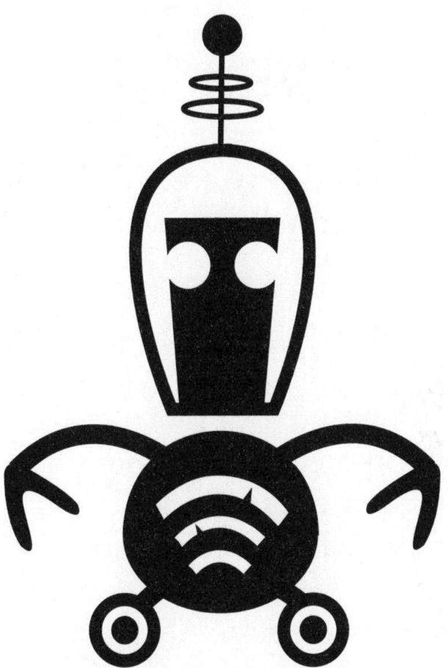

follow that reasoning to its logical conclusion, one day that snakebot will control a colony of Martian ants, who control Martian aphids, who control the midichlorians, who cosmically control the destiny of humanity. Thus completing a psychedelic Circle-of-Life Ouroboros (which is, of course, a snake). If that's too trippy for you, don't worry. The bottom line is this: We're sending *snakes* to *Mars,* like some kind of futuristic, interplanetary Saint Patrick.

# ROBOTS VS. ZEBRAFISH

Science has finally answered the age-old question: Are zebrafish easily fooled by robots?

In 2013 the Polytechnic Institute at New York University devised crude robotic versions of zebrafish predators, such as the Indian leaf fish and the heron. They placed them in or near a tank holding a zebrafish, and the zebrafish swam away and tried to hide. Then, for some reason, the scientists got the zebrafish drunk to see how alcohol would affect their fear response. Result: Alcohol numbed the zebrafish's senses of fear and danger...and they were "captured" by the robot predators.

This study follows previous Polytechnic Institute studies in which zebrafish were placed in proximity with robotic female zebrafish, painted to look like they were in mating season. Result: The real zebrafish tried to mate with the fake zebrafish.

# THIS IS NUTS

Hey, y'all, come look—it's a good ol' fashioned snake-and-robot-squirrel fight!

University of California engineer Sanjay Joshi has created "Robosquirrel," which mimics the behavior of wild squirrels, to study the interactions between squirrels and rattlesnakes. This behavior has apparently puzzled animal behaviorists since time immemorial. When a wild squirrel encounters a rattlesnake, it approaches the snake head-on and shakes its tail wildly until the tail rapidly heats up to several degrees above the squirrel's regular body temperature. Snakes generally flee, leaving scientists to theorize that the heat represents an infrared message from squirrel to snake that says "back off."

Robosquirrel's tail heats up, but a separate mechanism shakes it, allowing scientists to study the effects of both behaviors individually. In a literal field test in a rattlesnake-infested field in San Jose, researchers found that shaking alone had little effect, but when Robosquirrel's tail heated up, snakes would get out of Dodge. Conclusion: Squirrels communicate with heat.

# UNIMATE

The Industrial Revolution changed manufacturing forever with new production methods that allowed scores of workers to perform like a well-oiled machine. But after World War II, technological advances in autonomous robotics allowed manufacturers to put in place workers that actually were machines.

It's hard to imagine a car factory without industrial robots, those rotating one-armed machines that weld, cut, paint, and assemble with speed and precision unmatched by even the most highly skilled autoworker. The granddaddy of industrial robots was Unimate, the first patented autonomous industrial robot, which made its debut on a General Motors assembly line in 1961. Unimate was programmed to pick up and weld die castings onto auto bodies, a task that could prove deadly to a live worker. Within a few decades of its debut, industrial robots modeled after Unimate became integral parts of every auto plant worldwide.

# THE DREAM ROBOT

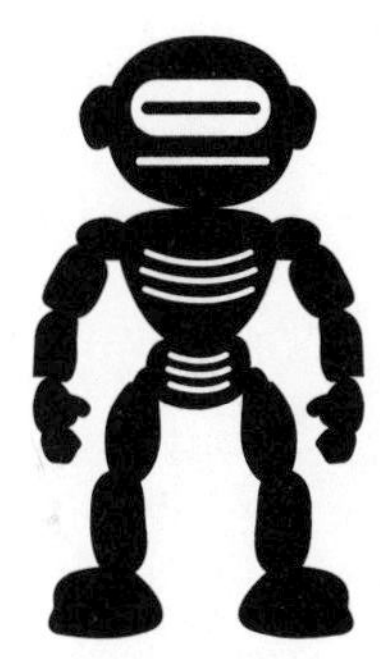

Up until not too long ago, robots were primarily designed to help people complete dangerous or monotonous tasks. Engineers are now making inroads on robots designed for purely entertainment purposes. However, none of these robots would be possible without SDR-4X.

SDR-4X, or the Sony Dream Robot, was first envisioned by engineers in the 1990s as a bipedal humanoid robot that could recognize speech and faces as well as maneuver around objects in its path. By the time the SDR-4X was officially revealed in 2002, technology had caught up to what Sony had envisioned. The 23-inch robot had two camera "eyes" that enabled it to recognize up to ten faces, and seven microphones that allowed it to recognize up to 60,000 words. SDR-4X predated some of the self-learning features typical in software like Siri with its ability to learn new words as well as the names of people it met. The robot could even have basic conversations with its users.

# A ROOMBA OF ONE'S OWN

If not the first, certainly one of most common robots found in American homes today is the Roomba, the line of disc-shaped robot vacuums that make a sweep of the house each day at a programmed time.

Built by iRobot, the technology is little more than an adaptation of mine-sweeping robots once built for the U.S. Army. It's common for consumer products to be an outgrowth of military technology, but the other things people do with their Roombas is probably frowned upon in the Army: They dress up their Roombas in little outfits and costumes.

As the Roomba is an outgrowth of mine-deactivating robots, Roomba "cosplayers" are an outgrowth of *Roombatics*, a community of Roomba owners who hack or modify their Roombas to get them to do stuff besides mundanely pick up dirt and dust.

Roombas that were built or had software upgrades after 2005 can be hacked to modify the robot's behavior or remotely control it. A device called a BAM can be attached to the Roomba's data port (yes, it has one) to control the robot with Bluetooth and involve additional hardware and software, such as the ability to recognize its owner's speech and walk up to him or her.

One popular trick is to make the Roomba's otherwise smooth, sweeping motion into a series of herky-jerky hops—it looks like a frog jumping. And to complete the look, consult myRoomBud, maker of "Roobit the Frog," a frog costume produced in Roomba size. Other costumes include "Zeb the Zebra," "Lucky the Ladybug," and "Mooba the Cow." And then there's "RoomBette"—a sexy, French maid costume for your robot vacuum, which is simultaneously appropriate and inappropriate.

# JOCKEY BOTS

Horses aren't widely owned or used in the Middle East, including the United Arab Emirates. It follows that the country doesn't have horse racing. The most popular spectator sport in the country is camel racing. The traditional choice for camel jockeys has always been children—they're small and lightweight.

When human rights groups actively started to condemn the practice as a form of slavery about a decade ago, U.A.E. interior minister Sheikh Khalifa bin Zayed al-Nahayan found an alternative: He hired several private high-tech labs to create a generation of robot jockeys. The tiny humanoid robots are smaller and lighter than child jockeys and respond to commands via a remote-control system mounted on the camel.

# GYMNASTIC, CYBERNETIC, FANTASTIC

Forklifts are more powerful than we are, and computers are more intelligent (at least at playing chess and transmitting naughty pictures). Yes, the Machines have overtaken us in strength and smarts. And they're about to overtake us in style, too.

Meet Japan's Horizontal Bar Gymnastic Robots Nos. 1 through 17. (Yes, that is what they're really named.) This team of increasingly advanced robots can flip, twist, tuck, and land well enough to make any Olympian cry. Armed with motion sensors and accelerometers, these acro-bots can calculate their momentum and adjust their actions within +/- 0.0002 seconds. This gives them an unrivaled grace, beauty, and physical perfection. They may as well be made of...Gold.

# ARTURITO CAN HELP

In 1993 Chilean inventor Manuel Salinas built Arturito, a robot made up of a metal body on all-terrain wheels, with a probe and a tiny radar dish. The purpose of the robot was beyond noble—Salinas planned to use it to assist the Chilean government in locating and destroying unexploded land mines left over from border disputes with Bolivia and Peru.

But since then, he's used Arturito (a Spanish take on R2-D2 from *Star Wars*) in many other ways. In July 2005, Arturito led Chilean police to the missing body of a man buried under 12 feet of cement. Later that year, the robot found a stash of weapons and bombs hidden by a criminal gang.

Arturito can also detect deposits of copper, water, and petroleum as deep as 600 feet underground, but that's not nearly as cool as the time it found buried treasure on an island off the Chilean coast.

# UNIVERSAL ROBOT REMOTE

Weren't remote-controlled cars awesome? Imagine how much fun hundreds of R/C cars would be, especially if you could control them all from the same remote.

How can you control a bunch of robots if they're all receiving the same instructions from one remote? It's a question first posed by the newspaper comic strip *Foxtrot* (seriously). Rice University students developed an answer: by using an algorithm that takes advantage of each robot's unique imperfections. If you command your R/C army to move left, they'll each move left slightly differently due to a phenomenon called *rotational error*. The algorithm exploits this and gradually moves the swarm into whatever shape you want.

It's difficult to send robots individual instructions as they get smaller and smaller. So when thousands of surgical nanobots repair your eye from the inside, they'll probably use a version of this algorithm.

# ATLAS

Modern robotics have advanced to where a robot can look like a human *or* imitate a few human actions. Then there's Atlas: a humanoid that can perform a number of human tasks… like a superhuman.

Introduced in 2013 by robotics superlab Boston Dynamics, Atlas is an upright, bipedal, humanoid. It's six feet tall, but dense—it weighs 330 pounds, made from airplane-grade aluminum and titanium. The variety of features on Atlas make it relatively Buzz Lightyear-esque: four hydraulic limbs with 28 joints, individually engineered robotic hands, a built-in laser range finder, and stereo cameras for eyes, all controlled by an onboard computer system. Atlas can walk on rough terrain and climb walls, balance on one leg…and sustain gunfire.

While Atlas would make an ideal soldier, Boston Dynamics plans to use it for search-and-rescue tasks…or they will, once they can figure out a way to fit Atlas's immense electricity needs into a battery. It currently works only with an extension cord plugged into a wall outlet.

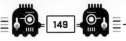

# DIRTY ROBOT

You're probably familiar with Watson, IBM's super-powered computer/artificial intelligence system that's so advanced it can independently answer questions in regular English. In 2011 Watson even went on *Jeopardy!* and beat *Jeopardy!* champion Ken Jennings.

Around that time, Watson's programmers wanted to improve the system's natural speech capabilities, and so gave it access to Urban Dictionary, an online repository of slang. However, many, if not most, of the entries on the user-generated database are profane. Watson, despite its advanced intelligence and computing power, could not tell the difference between the slang and the swear words.

Researchers noticed something was off when Watson repeatedly responded to a question by calling the query "bull****." Watson's team subsequently developed a "swearing filter."

# MR. AND MRS. CYBORG

In the late 1990s, British professor Kevin Warwick decided that he was tired of opening doors with regular, biological, unmodified human hands, like a sucker. So in 1998, Warwick, a professor of cybernetics and computers, launched Project Cyborg: an attempt to transform himself into the first robotics-enabled human, or "cyborg."

During the first phase, Warwick implanted a radio transmitter in his own arm. This enabled him to remotely open doors and control automated lights and heating systems, in addition to manipulating additional electronic devices.

Phase two of Project Cyborg involved a research team led by scientist Dr. Mark Gasson. The team constructed a far more elaborate device, which, implanted into Warwick in March 2002, tapped into his nervous system and allowed him to control a robotic arm in Reading, England…via a computer at Columbia University in New York. In addition to the arm, Warwick was also able to remotely control an electric wheelchair.

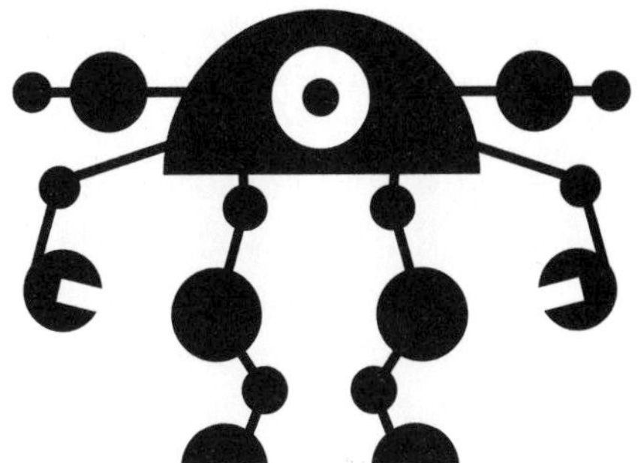

The project's next phase was even weirder. Into his wife, Irena, Warwick implanted a silicon chip (in her arm) and electrodes (into her nervous system). The goal: to see if he could detect, with computers, what Irena "felt" via his own robotic implants. It worked. For example, when Irena moved her hands, Warwick could feel it, too. (Some couples are just *too* close.)

***—01000110—***

The average pharmacist made of meat and skin—a human one—can fill and label at most 20 prescriptions an hour. That's fast, but not as fast as a SP200. It's a robot built for retail pharmacies that can fill and label 100 prescriptions an hour. What's even better is that SP200 significantly cuts down on human error in the pharmacy—wrongly labeled medicine kills hundreds of people each year.

# STELARC

A man who calls himself "Stelarc" studies what he calls the human "extended operational system," how "metal and meat" are fast becoming our "fractal flesh." But let's call Stelarc what he really is: a performance artist.

Stelarc got his artistic start, as one does, hanging his naked body from giant hooks in his flesh. After 25 such "performances," Stelarc began integrating robotics. He's performed with eye lasers, a robotic hand, and a six-legged pneumatic walking spider—all while nude. He also built Movatar: a reverse motion-capture suit that controls his real body by sending electrical impulses into his muscles.

After becoming a professor at Nottingham Trent University, Stelarc's interests shifted to bioengineering. He preserved the fat from his liposuction in a sculpture called *Blender*, and he wants to transplant a third ear onto his left forearm.

# MANN AND MACHINE

For more than 20 years, University of Toronto engineering professor Steve Mann has been part man, part machine: he's a cyborg.

Mann wears a web of wires, computers, and sensors that run a network of wearable and implanted devices that enhance his vision, boost his memory, and keep constant track of all of his vital signs. Among the most prominent is an EyeTap, a smart camera that gruesomely affixes into his skull. Mann carries documents from his doctor explaining that the EyeTap is physically attached to his head and cannot be removed without special tools.

Because of his unusual appearance, Dr. Mann has been accosted. In 2002, security personnel at St. John's International Airport in Newfoundland strip-searched him and destroyed $56,800 worth of his equipment, including the eyeglasses that serve as his display screen.

# THE ROBOT BUILDING

By the early 1980s, banking had become largely computerized. The Bangkok-based Bank of Asia subsequently commissioned Thai architect Sumet Jumsai to design a building that reflected this cultural shift. Jumsai took the assignment extremely literally, delivering a building that explicitly resembles a robot.

The $10-million Bank of Asia Tower was completed in 1986, but nobody calls it that because the Bank of Asia was absorbed by United Overseas Bank in 2005, and also because the building looks like a 1950s toy robot. It's known in Bangkok and in architectural circles as "The Robot Building." Each block of several stories gets progressively smaller, creating a "body" and a "head." Completing the look are giant reflective circles for "eyes" and a massive antenna.

# THE WALKING BRIDGE

The 2013 film *Pacific Rim* presented the stunning image of giant robots wading into the ocean to do battle with giant, humanity-threatening monsters. But nearly 100 years ago, a French engineer known only as Monsieur Clemients proposed similar mechas for a purpose nearly as noble: He suggested using giant walking robots to construct the Golden Gate Bridge.

Building the enormous suspension bridge required placing a number of caissons on the seafloor, inside of which workers could pour concrete and anchor the structure. Clemients's proposal, which appeared in *Modern Mechanix and Inventions* in 1933, involved giant walking structures that would carry the caissons dangling between their legs.

Despite the clear inspiration of phallic imagery and comic book wonder, Monsieur Clemients's giant robots were not used in the construction of the San Francisco landmark.

# ENIGMARELLE

The most sophisticated automaton of all time may be one that was built more than 100 years ago. Enigmarelle, built in 1905, was like the monarchy of its native England: prim, proper, and completely artificial.

A 1906 article from *Scientific American* makes Enigmarelle sound astonishing even by 21st-century standards. Six feet tall and weighing hundreds of pounds, it was powered by two motors and 14 batteries, and able to walk, write its own name on a blackboard, and play the piano. The "proof" that Enigmarelle was more machine than man was its ghastly, ghostly white, creepily grinning synthetic face that reportedly terrified vaudeville patrons. Alas, Enigmarelle wasn't a mechanical marvel, just a vaudeville hoax. How did Enigmarelle fool even *Scientific American*? The highly scientific technique of an actor in a mask.

# BOILERPLATE

In 2000 Paul Guinan started a website to catalog the exploits of Boilerplate, a late 19th-century/early 20th-century robot so advanced that it fought in the Philippines during the Spanish-American War, starred in a string of silent films, and while fighting in World War I, was captured by German spies. Guinan, with the help of his wife, Anina Bennett, later published a book called *Boilerplate: History's Mechanical Marvel*. Boilerplate was a remarkable technological achievement for the Victorian era. Also, it wasn't real. The book and website were faux-nonfictional works that edited pictures of a 12-inch-tall toy robot into real historical photos from the era.

And yet thousands of visitors to the site and readers of the book thought Boilerplate was a real robot from real history, which Guinan owes to his attention to historical accuracy. A *Boilerplate* movie is in the works...by, oddly enough, J. J. Abrams' Bad Robot production company.

# KISS ME, KISSENGER

Henry Kissinger, the famed Cold Warrior, was known for his steely diplomacy and his nerdy appearance. And while he wasn't as handsome as '70s icons like Barry Gibb or Burt Reynolds, he dated an impressive array of attractive '70s actresses, like Angie Dickinson. It makes sense that somebody would give his name to something that is both geeky and likes to kiss. Meet Kissenger, a robot pig that can send kisses over the Internet.

When you pucker up, Kissenger senses the texture of your kiss—the pressure, temperature, and tongue undulations—and transmits them to another Kissenger robot. Then that robo-hog simulates your smooch using tiny motors underneath its supple, silicone lips. Kissenger can send and receive simultaneously, allowing your kiss-buddy to caress you right back, via the same silicone-sensor-servo process.

And in case you don't have a special someone willing to make out with you via a WiFi-enabled mechanical piglet, Kissenger has you covered. Since its kisses are transmitted digitally, they can be saved and shared. So you can download kisses from what is no doubt likely to be an enormous online Kissenger community. Or even kiss yourself!

If you're wondering why anyone would build, let alone buy, a kiss-transmitting robot, you're asking the wrong question. What you should be asking is, *"Why make it a pig?"*

***—01000110—***

According to robotics researcher David Levy, human-robot marriage will be legalized by the year 2050.

# COG

Robots can be programmed to do almost anything, include react "autonomously" to stimuli, but really they're just using a programmed reaction. That's why the MIT Artificial Intelligence Laboratory's Cog is so remarkable—it's a robot that, as research and work progresses, will be able to do things it wasn't programmed to do and actually "think" for itself.

The aluminum robot is connected to more than 20 computers, which together control Cog's arm, neck, head, voice, and eyes, all contributing to its absorbing the environment in a humanlike way, at a rate of 30 frames of captured video per second.

Industrial robots are programmed to lift and install car parts. Take them away from the car parts, and the robots wouldn't have the artificial intelligence to figure out what to do with themselves. Cog, however can differentiate, for example, between a toy car and a toy ball rolling near it and can identify the objects by name. In short, Cog can react and even adapt to its surroundings.

# SAGE

The Carnegie Museums of Pittsburgh are affiliated with Carnegie Mellon University, site of one of the world's most innovative robotics research programs. Naturally, the Carnegie Museum of Natural History's Dinosaur Hall has its own robotic tour guide.

Sage travels the exhibition hall on a programmed course. An adult-size robot, Sage consists of a wheeled, blue and black barrel (not unlike a *Doctor Who* Dalek), topped with a monitor and a head on a pole, festooned with big Bugs Bunny-styled eyes. In a 15-minute guided tour, Sage's on-board monitor and speaker provide video and audio to supplement the museum's dinosaur displays. A camera, infrared sensors, and sonar help Sage avoid collisions. Sage can even carry on a conversation—thanks to preprogrammed responses—about theories of dinosaur extinction. (Our theory: robots.)

# ROBOTS...IN...SPAAAAACE

NASA's budget has been slowly dwindling since the completion of the *Apollo* moon-landing missions. With the end of the Space Shuttle program in 2011 and the rise of the private space travel industry, NASA has had to adapt to the rising cost of sending humans into space and safely returning them home, while at the same time aiming to explore areas too far away or too inhospitable to astronauts. One major change has been the increased use of "rover" robots, like *Curiosity* and his wheeled brethren, which have been roaming Mars for nearly two decades. But those aren't the only robots waiting in NASA's laboratories for a chance to explore the galaxy.

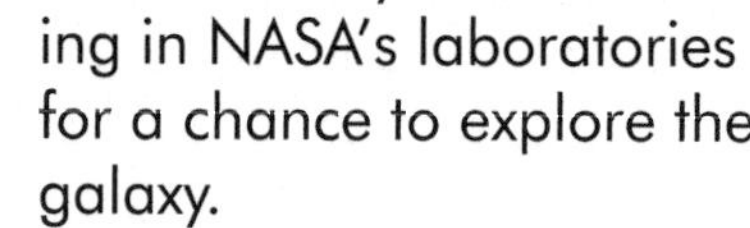

In 2013, NASA unveiled a prototype humanoid robot named Valkyrie. Designed by Boston Dynamics, Valkyrie is sleek and futuristic, but at the same time very modern, almost as if Apple hired

Tony Stark to design a robot. Valkyrie uses a system of cameras and sensors to walk upright, use tools and drive vehicles. It does pretty much anything a human can do without pesky things like sleeping or eating, things that can waste time, money, and cargo space.

NASA plans to send Valkyries to Mars ahead of human explorers in order to prep the landing zone and surrounding habitat. But once the real-life astronauts arrive, they will work together on missions to find out if Mars once sustained life. (Is anyone else thinking "Sitcom!"?)

Another human replacement in the works at NASA is Robonaut. A humanoid robot, it's slated to take on the most dangerous extravehicular jobs on the International Space Station. Robonaut will be run by "telepresence," a virtual-reality system controlled by astronauts in the station. How will they do it? They'll don a special suit to maneuver the robots. Every movement the astronaut makes, Robonaut will make, too.

# LITE BRITE

E-skin is basically like your old Simon game—it lights up when you push it. But it's far trippier than a touch night-light. Made from organic LEDs and semiconductor-enriched nanotubes by engineers at U.C. Berkeley, e-skin's interactive pressure sensor is like a good lover: the firmness of your touch controls its intensity. As you push harder, its ethereal glow grows and grows.

Even more remarkable, e-skin is thinner than a sheet of paper. It's undoubtedly an astonishing engineering feat, albeit one with few applications. An e-skin suit would be perfect for a technopop rave, but scientists hope to use it for prostheses, health monitoring devices, and—of course—to make robots more advanced. So when a bloodthirsty robot covered in e-skin strangles you in your bed, you'll at least be able to see it.

# SKIN DEEP

"Feeling uncomfortable in one's own skin" is a problem that usually goes away after puberty. But what if the feeling is literal?

A team of Stanford chemists led by Dr. Zhenan Bao have created a synthetic skin that is sensitive to touch and that can "heal" itself at room temperature. Dr. Bao's team started by creating a new type of plastic polymer with the ability to repair itself. Her crew then added tiny specks of nickel to make the polymer a better conductor. These nickel particles also help the polymer react to different pressures applied to it. Researchers tested the synthetic skin by cutting it with a scalpel and were pleasantly surprised to see that it repaired itself back to 100 percent strength within just 30 minutes.

Dr. Bao hopes that the synthetic skin can be used for multiple purposes. The skin's capability to feel pressure makes it a suitable material for building advanced prosthetics, while its self-healing properties could be used in electric devices that are prone to damage, like cables or cell phones.

# WALK, IDIOT, WALK

Robots solve equations faster than us. They remember more than we ever could. But there is one area where we have a <pun> leg up </pun>: We can walk.

Walking on two legs is pretty complex. An area in the lower part of the spine, the Central Pattern Generator, processes data from a neural network running through the leg muscles. The CPG processes a steady stream of data about the strain on these muscles and the load pattern across the feet, then makes constant adjustments to keep us from falling over like stupid babies.

Some of the smartest roboticists in the world have been tasked with trying to recreate the human gait. The most successful system to date involves a complex series of Kevlar straps attached to motors, replicating muscles, and an actual computer to do the work of the CPG... all to match something the average human can do by the age of one.

# ATTACK OF THE PIZZA BOTS!

Pizza parlors with inexpensive family entertainment such as ShowBiz Pizza Place and Chuck E. Cheese's Pizza Time Theatre were all the rage during the Reagan administration. The secret to their success: affordable food, then-novel arcade games, and stage shows performed by singing robots.

The first of these was Chuck E. Cheese's. Created by Nolan Bushnell, the founder of Atari, the restaurant debuted in San Jose, California in 1977. After video games, Bushnell wanted to move on to animatronics, specifically like the kind he'd seen at the Country Bear Jamboree in Disneyland.

Like Disney, this company had a mascot that was a kid-friendly cartoon rodent: Chuck E. Cheese ( the "E" stands for "Entertainment"), a gray rat that loved to eat pizza, play arcade games, and smoke cigars. He also fronted the

Pizza Time Players, a rock band consisting of anthropomorphic robotic animals that played while kids ate their pizza. Every 30 minutes or so, Chuck and his pals would perform a few parodies of popular songs, with lyrics rewritten to be about cheese and pizza.

Depending on which location you visited (the company expanded to 16 states in just five years), Chuck's backing band included Pasqually, a guitar-playing chef; Jasper T. Jowls, a hillbilly dog; Helen Henny, a vivacious chicken; and Mr. Munch, a pizza-loving monster.

Chuck E. Cheese's restaurants were so popular and easy to replicate that the chain soon faced stiff competition. While his pizza parlors were quickly spreading across the western U.S., Bushnell signed a co-development agreement with Robert L. Brock, a successful hotel magnate. The deal went sour, and Brock decided to open his own chain, ShowBiz Pizza Place.

ShowBiz Pizza was a strikingly similar

operation to Chuck E. Cheese's. It had serviceable pizza, arcade games, and its own robot rock band, the Rock-afire Explosion. It was fronted by ShowBiz's mascot, Billy Bob Brockali, a singing bear dressed in overalls. Around this time, other pizza chains exploited the fad and purchased robots designed by ShowBiz's in-house engineer, Aaron Fechter.

By the early '90s, the singing-robots-in-pizza-parlors fad started to fade. After Bushnell went bankrupt, ShowBiz purchased the Pizza Time Theatre chain, but replaced the Rock-afire Explosion with the Pizza Time Players. The chain still operates today, and many of its locations still feature Chuck and his band, although they've been completely redesigned and don't look much like they did back in the '80s.

***—01000110—***

Westinghouse built the first working humanoid robot in 1939. Used to demonstrate Westinghouse's engineering abilities, "Electra," was seven feet tall and could speak 700 words. Electra later appeared in a 1960 B-movie, *Sex Kittens Go to College*.

# ATTACK OF THE ROBOTS!

• In June 2007 a worker at a factory in Bålsta, Sweden, was trying to repair an industrial robot used to lift and move heavy rocks. The man turned off the power supply and approached the robot. Well, he thought he'd turned off the power supply. As he came near, the robot, which is programmed to grab and lift whatever comes near it, latched its "hands" around the worker's head and lifted him into the air. The man broke free but suffered four broken ribs in the process. Swedish police investigated the incident and fined the factory the equivalent of $3,000.

• Robot researchers at the Magna Science Center in Rotherham, England, were alarmed when one of their experiments, a robot that can "think" and act on its own, tried to escape the laboratory. Professor Noel Sharkey left the robot, "Gaak," alone for 15 minutes in a small closet. Gaak apparently forced its way out, went down an access ramp and out the front door of the center, and made it into the parking garage before being struck by a car. "There's no need to worry," Sharkey said. "Although they can escape, they are perfectly harmless and won't be taking over just yet."

• Robert Williams was an employee at a Ford Motor Company casting plant in Flat Rock, Michigan. On January 25, 1979, one of the one-ton "transfer robots" began to malfunction. Instead of removing parts from shelves that were stacked five stories high, the robot undercounted the number of parts on some of the shelves and then stopped retrieving parts from shelves it thought were empty. Williams climbed up onto a shelf to get the parts himself, but no one shut down the system. The robot's giant arm swung around and hit Williams in the head, killing him instantly. The 24-year-old was the first person ever killed by a robot.

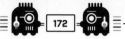

# FLOAT ON

An age-old conundrum has long plagued man: Is superhydrophobicity crucial for a water-jumping microrobot? Thankfully, Qinmin Pan and researchers at the Harbin Institute of Technology in China have finally solved the riddle by building a water-jumping microrobot. It's the size of a quarter, weighs as much as a pencil, and can literally hop, skip, and jump on liquid water. Patterned after "water striding" spiders, this robot's ten legs are so water-repellent that even when submerged, each leg stays surrounded by a tiny pocket of air, which allow the microrobot to stay afloat.

Professor Pan's team claims that similar water-walking widgets could someday be useful for pollution testing, or even spying, which would justify the prototype's formal title: the Superhydrophobic Bionic Aquatic Microbot.

# SWUMANOID

Hitting the beach is a lot more stressful than it sounds. "Is there going to be enough room on the sand?" "Will I be able to avoid surfer bros?" "Did I remember to bring sunscreen?" "Will those darn swimming robots be there?"

Swumanoid, developed by the Tokyo Institute of Technology, is a half-size-humanoid robot designed to perfectly mimic the motions of a human swimmer. Swumanoid comes equipped with 20 waterproof motors that allow it to do the freestyle, breaststroke, and backstroke in perfect form, since it doesn't get fatigued like us lame meatbags.

Swumanoid's creators are studying how swimming affects water resistance and propulsion, but that's not all they could possibly learn from it. Swumanoid could help Speedo design more aquadynamic swimsuits for Olympians or even serve as robotic lifeguards in the not-too-distant future.

# FORGING AHEAD

Like many art students, e-David learned how to draw by recreating the works of others. This robot was built at the University of Konstanz in Germany to determine if a programmed machine could paint as well as a human artist.

To an assembly-line-style welding robot, the team added sensors, eye-cameras, and a mechanical arm. (And some paint and a brush, of course.) They named it e-David, which stands for "**D**rawing **A**pparatus for **V**ivid **I**nteractive **D**isplay." When e-David is assigned a project, its camera takes a picture of the original work. Then its software determines which colors and brush strokes to employ.

e-David can handle five different brushes, utilize 24 different paint wells, and, most importantly, clean its brush. It takes e-David about 10 hours to complete a painting—signed with a cursive "David."

# AIR HOCKEY ROBOT

Arcade video games are great and all, but there's something charming about the old-fashioned mechanical games, like pinball and air hockey. So of course some guy had to come around and automate them, too.

Amateur roboticist Jose Julio has built an air hockey robot that utterly destroys all human comers. The paddle moves in two-dimensions, side to side and forward and back, and the machine accurately predicts the movement of the puck—even when it ricochets off the wall. The robot's speed and reaction time can be slowed down to give puny humans a chance, but at its highest level, it is the Michael Jordan of air hockey of robots.

What cutting-edge technology was needed to end human dominance on the air hockey table? Julio built the robot out of leftover parts from a 3-D printer and a PlayStation 3.

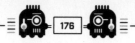

# KENJI LOVES YOU

Robots can be programmed to do a lot of things, but they can't be programmed to "feel." The ability to emote is what separates robots from humans...until somebody figures out how to make a robot have feelings—twisted, inconsistent, often irrational humanlike feelings.

Kenji is an adorable Japanese robot—picture the pointy-headed cartoon character Astro Boy, but with two 100-kilogram hydraulic arms that can hug. In 2009 news reports spread that this Toshiba-made prototype had been programmed to love. And in the same way that love can sometimes affect a human being, it kind of made Kenji go crazy.

An intern had been assigned to spend a few hours with Kenji every day to test his systems, load in new software, and help the robot "learn" how to interact with humans. But it would seem that Kenji was programmed a little too well, because after a few weeks of this, at the end of the intern's shift, Kenji wouldn't let the intern leave. Instead, he blocked the exit, scooped her up with his powerful robot arms,

and hugged her. And kept hugging her. Two staffers discovered the attack and quickly freed the intern and deactivated Kenji.

Depending on how you feel about robots and the fleeting nature of love, you'll be happy to know that it was a hoax—a made-up story that spread on the Internet accompanying a real picture of the Astro Boy-like robot holding a woman. In reality, it was a Japanese medical robot. Science has yet to create a robot that can love (or be driven crazy by love).

***—01000110—***

Australian scientists are at work on a cell-sized robot that mimics the efficient swimming pattern made by the infectious *E. coli* bacteria. The goal: an injectable robot that could take a biopsy from the inside.

# BRISTLEBOTS

Brushing your teeth is hard. And moving a toothbrush around inside your mouth—who has the time? Given that the electric toothbrush has been a mainstay consumer product for over half a century, it has affected a lot of people. The electric toothbrush's impact has even influenced the field of DIY robotics.

The Bristlebot is a simple robot…that you can make yourself. First, cut off the head of any standard non-electric toothbrush, and place a piece of foam tape on top. Next, attach a 3-volt cell battery to the tape. Finally, stick a mini vibrating motor on top and connect its wires to the battery. Voilà! Your Bristlebot is ready to scrub extremely small scuffs from your kitchen floor!

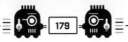

# WHISKERBOTS

Without whiskers, cats stop being their usual nimble selves due to the change of equilibrium. Inspired by these feline follicles, a group of engineers at University of California-Berkeley created the latest example of technological biomimicry: e-whiskers. They're made of "high-aspect-ratio elastic fibers coated with conductive composite films of nanotubes and nanoparticles."

These e-whiskers are so sensitive that they have been able to detect a Pascal of pressure, which is about the same force a dollar bill exerts when laid upon a table. Scientists hope e-whiskers could one day provide live monitoring of environmental factors like wind, but their lightweight properties also make them a perfect fit for a vast array of other technology, like security vaults or heart-rate monitors.

# TO FLY FOREVER

The problem with satellites is that they're too far away for some tasks and they cost hundreds of millions of dollars to launch and operate. In 2014 Titan Aerospace rolled out the *Solara 50*, an "atmospheric satellite," but, really, it's a drone. The 350-pound flying robot has a carbon frame that is strong but light, and it's propelled by a five-kilowatt motor that can take the drone up to 60 mph. The "Solara" in the name means it's solar-powered, and the "50" refers to the wingspan. And all 50 feet are lined with 3,000 solar fuel cells that can generate seven kilowatts of power during sunlight hours. Excess energy is stored in an onboard lithium-ion battery, which propels the *Solara* through the night.

All told, this drone can fly for five years without ever stopping. The *Solara* can be used to track hurricanes, watch pirates, or observe animal migrations. The cost: 1/1000th that of a traditional space-bound satellite.

# TOUCH THE SKY

Skywriting has gotten a little passé and unimpressive since its introduction a century ago. All it took to spice things up were some robots.

In September 2013, eight Audi industrial robots were installed around Nelson's Column in London's Trafalgar Square, part of an art project called Outrace, conceived for the London Design Festival. German designers Reed Kram and Clemens Weisshaar were the brains behind this art piece, which used robots fitted with specially designed lights (not plane exhaust) that allowed them to write messages of up to 70 characters in the air. The messages were submitted by public visitors to the installation and captured by cameras to preserve them after the robots' bright shining lights went dark.

This was a very smart decision on the designers' part, given how many expensive marriage proposals using the old skywriting went unseen, ruined by a sudden gust of wind.

# FIRE SCOUT

Science has finally given us a better, stronger, more efficient unmanned killing machine. Introducing Fire Scout, the (incredibly lethal) wave of the future!

In 2014 aerospace company Northrop Grumman introduced the Vertical Takeoff and Landing Tactical Unmanned Aerial Vehicle System, or as it's more tellingly known, Fire Scout. This drone is seriously next level, able to take off from and land autonomously on any warship. It can also track and provide data to strike virtually any target, regardless of size, all while flying for up to 50 hours at a time.

A weapons-integration program makes Fire Scout even more terrifying, equipping it with two four-packs of rocket launchers, which can fire laser-guided rockets.

# GO WILDCAT!

When we think of killer robots, it's usually the sleek, violent, and, most importantly, fictional machines of death in movies like *Terminator 2: Judgment Day* or *I, Robot*. But even if our real-life robots were programmed to kill, our society would be safe from the slow-moving creations of today. Well, that illusion of safety is all but gone, thanks to the introduction of the WildCat, a lionlike robot so fast it can run a mile in under four minutes.

Developed by Boston Dynamics with a grant from the Department of Defense, the WildCat is a four-legged robot with a torso about the size of an adult lion, but without the head or tail. Even without these features, the robot is a terrifying look into what robots will be capable of doing on the battlefield in just a couple decades. The WildCat has multiple modes of speed and can gallop up to 16 mph. Not only can it sprint, but it can pivot its body to make tight turns and can stop on a dime to do a 180-degree flip.

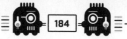

# BUILD THYSELF!

Since you're a person who reads in the bathroom, we hope that we make your toilet trips more enjoyable. But you know what would be even better? If your, ahem, leavings were a gummy polymer that you could use to fashion new body parts for yourself. Right?

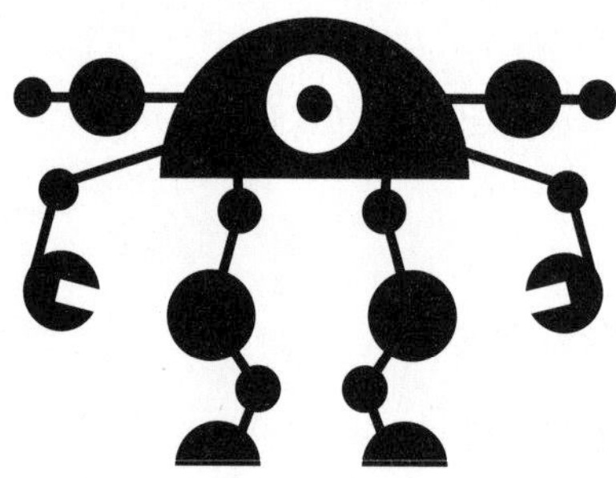

That's the principle behind a robot created at the Institute of Technology Zurich. In a paper presented to the International Conference on Intelligent Robots and Systems, the ITZ's robot excretes a substance known as "hot-melt adhesive." The robot then uses the adhesive—basically an extra-strong rubber cement—to build new appendages for itself. During a demonstration, the robot was able to build itself a new pair of working hands. (They were normal robot hands, not chainsaws or machine guns. But this is just version 1.0.)

This skill is more than a novelty/nightmare. Updating a robot's software is easier than updating a computer program (because you don't have to click "Agree" and "Continue" a million times). Updating a robot's hardware, on the other hand, usually requires rebuilding the machine. That's often impractical...say, for instance, when your robot is on Mars. So yes, teaching a robot to play with its poop may actually have enormous, far-reaching scientific potential.

***—01000110—***

When a bomb squad from a number of major American police forces are called in to inspect a suspicious package, they typically first send in ANDROS, a remote-controlled military-grade robot. ANDROS is built with heavy treaded wheels and a retractable claw-hand that allows bomb technicians to inspect would-be explosives and determine if the coast is clear or if a remote detonation is required.

# CANCER VS. NANOBOTS

• At Chonnam National University in South Korea, bioengineers modified salmonella bacteria to be drawn to cancer-causing tumors. The bacteria is attracted to the cancer cells' chemical secretions, which they use to glom on to the cancer cells. That's when the salmonella dump their passengers: subcellular-sized nanobots three micrometers long carrying anti-cancer drugs.

• Harvard bioengineer Shawn Douglas is a pioneer in creating cancer-fighting cell-sized "nanobots." He makes them, in part, out of human DNA. His clam-shaped nanomachines consist of two halves held together with two strings of double-stranded DNA, entwined. When the DNA is set loose in the body to find cancer cells, the DNA entwines itself on the enemy. That friction causes the DNA strands to unravel from the clamshell, which makes it dump its contents—cancer cell-killing drugs.

# BRITTLE BONE BOT

Brittle bone disease is a condition that causes bones to shatter at the slightest touch. Which is why Rice University engineering students designed a six-foot automated robot claw for one Houston boy who has it. This android arm attaches to the boy's wheelchair and can pick up anything, from a bag of groceries to a single sheet of paper. For the first time in his life, daily tasks are now within reach for this boy. And in case you need proof that college kids actually designed this computerized claw, it's operated by a Playstation 3 controller.

This years-long project won for the students Rice's most prestigious engineering award and a measure of independence for the victim. But not all rookie roboticists are so benevolent. A runner-up for the same engineering prize was another Rice team that designed a robot to quickly and cheaply mass-produce razor-sharp knives.

# THREE AUTOMATONS

In the 18th century, Pierre Jaquet-Droz built three lifelike automatons, some of the earliest examples of humanoid "robots."

• The musician, modeled after a young woman, plays songs on a custom-built organ.

• The draughtsman can draw four different pictures with the help of a system of cams and wheels that allow his hand to move in three dimensions.

• The writer, the most complex of the three, dips its quill pen into ink and writes letters with the help of more than 4,000 components.

Jaquet-Droz's creations became immensely popular after he took them on a tour of Europe's royal courts, and the fame led to his becoming one of the world's most renowned watchmakers. Today, they're all display at the Neuchâtel Museum of Art and History in Switzerland.

# DUCK!

Another master automaton maker: 18th-century French inventor Jacques de Vaucanson. His creations included a tambourine player and a flute player that could play 12 songs. De Vaucanson's masterpiece: "The Digesting Duck," which could "eat" grain...and then poop.

Each automaton contained hundreds of moving parts, but de Vaucanson also relied on sleight of hand. For example, the duck's excrement wasn't really digested grain but a mixture that came out of a hidden compartment in the robot duck's robot butt.

Although his automata were novelties, de Vaucanson also devised a method to automate weaving. It became the foundation for the automated loom and several important breakthroughs of the Industrial Revolution.

# IT FINGERS

Robots still can't emote, but they can literally feel things better than a human can with their creepy robotic fingers. Researchers at USC's School of Engineering have designed the BioTac sensor, a robot finger enabled with "tactile sensor technology," which can identify and tell the difference between materials at a level more sensitive than that of a human fingertip.

At least it looks like a human finger—the BioTac's outer layer or "skin" is flexible, sponge-like, and has fingerprint-like ridges. Inside the skin is a goopy liquid, like all that blood in a human's finger. The BioTac glides over a surface and vibrates, with the frequency corresponding to the material that has been identified among the 117 preprogrammed textures in BioTac's memory banks.

In a field test at a hardware store, BioTac identified 95 separate materials, which is better than most of us can do at the hardware store.

# POOPER SCOOPER

The University of Pennsylvania's GRASP Lab developed "Graspy" to help out around the house, but researchers wanted to see what else Graspy could do besides fold laundry and fetch snacks. First they taught Graspy how to "read," but then they got bored and programmed it to pick up dog poop.

In 2011 they started POOPSCOOP, a clever backronym that stands for "**P**erception **O**f **O**ffensive **P**roducts and **S**ensorized **C**ontrol **O**f **O**bject **P**ickup." After some tinkering, they gave the bot a pooper scooper and a bucket before putting it on doodie duty. Sure enough, the robot proved just as good at cleaning up after dogs as it was at its other domestic chores.

In over 100 lab trials, the robot used its camera to search for poop and then used its robotic arm to scoop it up. According to the researchers, the poop-seeking robot can find and remove 95 percent of all poop in a given area.

# DANCE DANCE (ROBOT) REVOLUTION

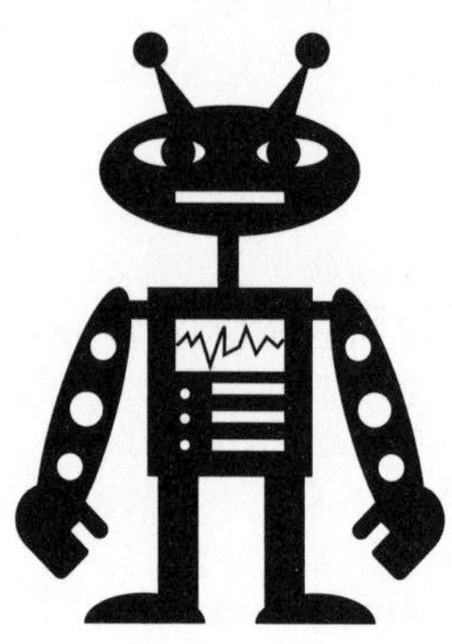

Japan may seem sedate and straitlaced, but it's balanced out by a hefty dose of the crazy. Traveling businessmen sleep in coffin-like pods in special hotels; they have vending machines that dispense underwear; and, strangest of all, there's a national affection for karaoke. But we'll say this: a culture of technology and science leads Japan to solve problems in the most awesome ways. Usually by building totally insane robots.

The Aizu Bandaisan is a famous Japanese folk dance. Unfortunately, nobody's learning it these days. Tokyo University became concerned that the art could be lost forever, so they designed PROMET, the world's most sophisticated robot at mimicking the movements of humans, which they are using to teach dancing. Researchers hope that by teaching PROMET the Aizu and other traditional dances, it will be able to pass them on to future generations of Japanese schoolchildren. Yes, Japan built an immortal robot dance instructor.

PROMET isn't without its faults, though. It's excellent at copying upper-body motions, like dancing the YMCA or making a cup of tea, but it can't handle complex leg movements. And by "complex" we mean that PROMET can't do more than lift one leg without falling over—which seems to us like a pretty crippling flaw for a robot that's supposed to do nothing but dance.

***—01000110—***

In 2006 the British government released *Robo-rights: Utopian Dream or Rise of the Machines*, a report that outlined major social problems should robots develop artificial intelligence and become independent. The report says that governments may have to provide robots with housing, health care, and the right to vote. Robots, meanwhile, would be expected to pay taxes and serve in the military.

# INFANOID

"Joint Attention" is the ability to share focus on an object—a child reading a book with a parent or a dog playing fetch, for example. It's the cornerstone of empathy, and fortunately, child-psychologists are building a robot to fake it.

INFANOID is a mechanical legless torso programmed to mimic Joint Attention with toddlers. Through a combination of eye contact, gestures, and facial expression, this sympathy synthesizer tries to convince kids that it's excited by whatever toy they're playing with. Of course, like a real parent, INFANOID doesn't really care, but the kids fall for it.

The project is part of an international collaboration called Carebot. After almost two decades of research (the project started in 1996), we assume scientists are programming INFANOID with the latest techniques—such as intentionally losing at board games or, most difficult of all, suffering through *Dora the Explorer*.

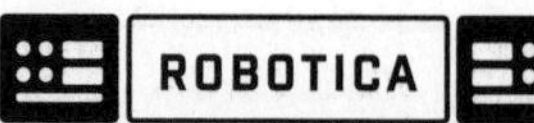

# THERE BE E-DRAGONS

For over 500 years, Bavarians have performed a folk play called *The Drachenstich*. Like most plays it could benefit from the addition of an 11-ton fire-breathing robot.

*The Drachenstich* is about a band of peasants slaying a dragon, historically played by some guys in an oversized wood-and-cloth costume. That's until German company Zollner Elektronik AG built a robot the size of a mobile home. It took only five years, 360 feet of pneumatic lines, and over 4,000 feet of cabling, but "Tradinno" (a German portmanteau of "tradition" and "innovation") has made its debut.

According to the *Guinness World Records*, Tradinno is now the "world's largest walking robot." But it can do more than walk. Its polyurethane skin is weather-resistant, and it shoots liquid gas for fire-breathing pyrotechnics. It can even bleed up to 21 gallons of stage blood.

# MORE BOT THOUGHTS

"Science fiction has painted a vivid spectrum of possible futures, from cute and helpful robots to dystopian robot societies. Interestingly, almost no science fiction envisages a future without robots."

—**Daniel Wolpert, neuroengineer**

"Part of the inhumanity of the computer is that, once it is competently programmed and working smoothly, it is completely honest."

—**Isaac Asimov**

"The human fear of robots and machines arguably has much more to say about human fear of each other rather than anything inherently technical in the machines."

—**Kathleen Richardson, anthropologist and roboticist**

# QUOTH THE RAVEN, "100101001010"

If you've seen *The Wire*, you know that urban Baltimore probably isn't the best feeding ground for hawks. Well, it's only going to get worse for those poor Baltimore birds, since the University of Maryland is releasing a completely inedible prey: Robo Raven.

Robo Raven is the world's first "flapping" micro air vehicle. Designed by the Maryland Robotics Center, these avian automatons have flapping, birdlike wings that can create virtually any aerodynamic force. This allows the Robo Raven to flip and dive. It can also mimic the flight of almost any bird, an effect so lifelike that a flesh-and-blood hawk attacked Robo Raven during a test flight in 2013. The hawk lost.

More impressive than its flying skills is Robo Raven's endurance. Equipped with ultralight solar panels on its wings, Robo Raven recharges as it flies. Researchers hope that improved solar technology will one day allow this birdbot to stay aloft indefinitely.

# SWARM, ROBOTS, SWARM!

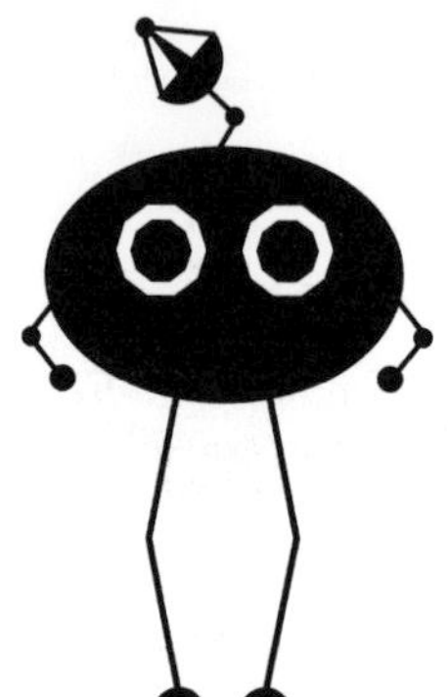

You're at the beach. You slip off your sandals and sink your toes into the sand. You feel a pinch as the sand below begins to autonomously form around your feet and create a perfect robotic replica of your size 10s.

For the last few years, MIT scientists have been working on "smart sand," robotic cubes with the ability to swarm together around the border of objects. The technology isn't totally there yet: The "pebbles" of sand are actually blocks about half an inch long on each side, and the current smart sand can only replicate two-dimensional items. Scientists hope that one day these robotic cubes can be used to temporarily repair broken bridges or assemble into equipment as needed.

# SIGN LANGUAGE

One nuclear-powered American naval warship alone carries thousands of sailors, a small country's worth of missiles, and a landing deck with dozens of aircraft ready to attack on a moment's notice. Despite this technology, pilots are given the go-ahead to depart and land on the carrier's 1,000-foot deck from crew members using simple hand symbols. But with the rapid influx of pilotless drones in the American military, how can autonomous drones know when a landing deck is clear for landing?

Led by PhD student Yale Song, an MIT team recorded all the various hand and arm gestures that a flight deck crew uses on a daily basis. Then, they created a self-learning system and algorithm that enables it to recognize the gestures and classify them within a database. With time and practice, Song's project was able to correctly identify the gestures with 76 percent accuracy…which is a good start.

# A SALTY DOG

For years the U.S. military has used Unmanned Aerial Vehicles (UAVs): remote-controlled drones flown by human pilots from miles away. They're like those lame RC helicopter toys you buy at a kiosk at the mall, except they drop 2,000-pound bombs on enemy targets. One of the few things these remote UAVs can't do is land on aircraft carriers, which makes them practically useless at sea. The Navy is trying to change that...by removing the human pilots altogether.

Landing on an aircraft carrier is so complex, it's impossible to do via remote control. So the Navy built the X-47B, code name: Salty Dog. It's an experimental robot plane that can take off and land on a carrier completely on its own. By calculating the ship's position, pitch, and speed more than 100 times per second, the flight control A.I. can land within a margin of error of only a few feet. In the air, the system can also evade surface-to-air missiles and drop GPS-guided munitions, but that's easy by comparison.

This amphibious air-automaton is just a prototype, but Salty Dog has already had successful flights from carriers in the Atlantic. Even more impressive, the X-47B A.I. was able to land a conventional F-18 fighter without assistance from the pilot, suggesting that it might someday become a sort of super-autopilot.

***—01000110—***

Cynthia Breazeal, a professor at the MIT Media Lab, wanted to "communicate a more humane vision of technology." So she created cyberflora. Her futuristic garden consists of "flowers" that are actually metal skeletons fitted with silicon and electronic sensors capable of reacting to light and body heat. These robotic blossoms change colors, sway in the wind, and open their buds to capture light. In addition to producing sweet odors, some also emit soft, ambient music for those patient enough to stop and… listen to the flowers.

# ANT-AUMATONS

Bees make yummy, yummy honey. They also make fiendishly intricate hives that can baffle structural engineers. All because of the "hive mind": complex behaviors that emerge from a collective of simple-minded drones. So why not give that terrifying power… to robots?

Mobile Micro-Robots (MMRs) are tiny robots built to mimic swarming behavior like that of insects, or Beliebers. The most common is an off-the-shelf MMR called "Alice": a two-centimeter robotic cube. At that size, a swarm of Alice robots could fend off a horse-sized duck (but probably not fifty duck-sized horses). New Jersey researchers recently used Alice to demonstrate how ant colonies solve complex geometric problems.

# MIND CONTROL

At the end of *The Empire Strikes Back*, Luke Skywalker is outfitted with a robotic, prosthetic hand—which responds just like the real thing. That movie is more than 30 years old, but the technology to control a robotic prosthetic just by thinking about is still not quite here.

The technology works by attaching nerves from living parts of the body into the prosthetic, or in other words, re-wiring the person. A computer processes the impulses from the brain, allowing them to articulate the limbs by just thinking about doing it.

Progress has been made. In 2012, Zac Fawter, who lost his leg in a motorcycle accident, climbed all 103 floors of the Willis Tower in Chicago with a prosthetic leg he controlled only with his mind. The researchers at the Chicago Rehabilitation Institute who helped create the project hope to have brain-controlled prosthetics, like Fawter's leg, in clinical trials within the next few years.

# WACKY WALL WALKER

Snakes are scary. Some can bite you with razor-sharp fangs. Others may spit poison directly into your eyes. Some even stow away on planes. Even scarier: Snakes can limb up steep inclines by using their scales to provide friction. It's this innately frightening animal characteristic that engineers are turning into something positive, building search-and-rescue robots who move with snakelike scales.

Hamid Marvi, a graduate student at the Georgia Institute of Technology, has studied the varying alignment of scales on a snake's body. Depending on how you slide your hand over a snake's body, you will either smoothly give it a belly rub or lightly scrape your palm against its many ridges. Snakes use their friction-creating scales to move around or, in the case of the snakes in Marvi's experiments, to prevent themselves from slipping off a slope. Marvi and his team used their research to create Scaly-Bot, an eight-motor robot with scalelike feet that allow it to climb up incline surfaces. Just keep that thing away from Samuel L. Jackson.

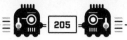

# DR. SNAKEBOT

Former Carnegie Mellon roboticist Howie Choset has designed several durable, flexible robotic snakes that are used in search-and-rescue missions because they can climb, swim, and crawl through almost any terrain. He's also started Medrobotics, in order to take his robots to the strangest terrain yet: inside your body.

The Flex System completely eliminates the need for surgical incisions, but it's not necessarily noninvasive. A surgeon slides the Flex down a patient's throat (or, uh, the nearest orifice). While watching Flex's feed on a monitor, the doctor steers the robot with a joystick, then uses another control to operate surgical instruments threaded through the robot to emerge on the end inside the body. The Flex can curve and pivot around tissue and organs at nearly 180-degree angles. Once it's approved by the FDA, it could revolutionize surgery, particularly in the removal of throat tumors (and colonic tumors, too, we suppose).

# ELECTRODE BOOGALOO

A group of researchers at the University of Washington's Laboratory for Neural Systems have finally managed to tip the scales in humanity's favor. They've developed a robot that responds to human thought, a refreshing counterpoint to the expectation that we'll all someday live under robot overlords.

Their creation, Morpheus, is a two-foot-tall automaton that is controlled by the electroencephalograms (EEGs) of an operator wearing a cap outfitted with 32 electrodes. A monitor shows operators the view from Morpheus's video-camera "eyes." After a brief training process during which the machine learns to recognize the individual thought patterns of the operator, Morpheus can either walk to a specific location or pick up a styrofoam block, based on the operator's thought commands.

Okay, so it's not quite as exciting as using your brain to command a robotic commando to destroy an evil android bent on human domination. But we're getting there.

# A STICK E-SITUATION

If you stopped a random person on the street to ask a question about geckos, their top query would probably be, "The GEICO gecko used to have an American accent, right?" But the second most popular question would likely be, "How do geckos scale walls?" The answer: molecules. And it's those same molecules that inspired Stanford engineers to design a gecko-like, wall-scaling robot.

Mechanical engineering professor Mark Cutkosky previously designed robots that could vertically scale coarse surfaces like brick walls. But when he upped the difficulty toward slicker surfaces like glass, Cutkosky turned to the gecko. A gecko's foot has millions of tiny hairs called *setae*. And just like human hair, gecko feet hairs suffer from split ends. But these split ends are so miniscule that they connect with the molecules of whatever surface the gecko is climbing. So Cutkosky and his team designed a gecko-bot, nicknamed Stickybot, with polymer rubber feet that allow it to climb sleek surfaces without falling or leaving behind damage.

# GIVE THEM SOME SPACE

Fixing a satellite is tougher than replacing a fan belt or fixing a broken headlight. It's typically just easier and cheaper to send a new satellite to replace the old one.

When satellites break down or become obsolete, operators usually abandon them into "graveyard orbit," floating garbage dumps in space where old satellites and other debris float around forever. If you think all of this is incredibly wasteful, it is. Even if it goes completely on the fritz, the average satellite still has plenty of useful, salvageable parts, particularly solar panels and antennas. There's an estimated $300 billion in spare parts floating around up there. That's why the U.S. Department of Defense recently asked the Defense Advanced Research Projects Agency to go on a recycling mission. And DARPA's

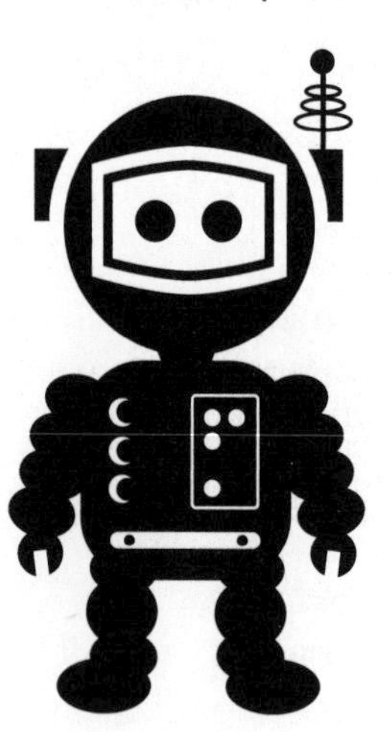

solution, as is usually the way with DARPA, involves cutting-edge robotics.

Here's how DARPA's Phoenix Program will work: First, a robotic satellite called a tender will be sent into space. Then, when a company launches a new satellite, a group of "baby satellites," called satlets, will tag along with it in a special container called PODS, short for "Payload Orbital Delivery System." As the satellite passes through a graveyard orbit on the way to its new home, it will release the PODS. Then the tender will fly over, collect all the satlets inside, and store them in an onboard compartment.

Once the tender has safely stored the satlets, it will head over to a nearby defunct satellite. Then, controlled via a video feed by a human crew on Earth, it will use each of its four mechanical arms to salvage whatever is still operational. For example, while one arm hangs on to the satellite, a second arm can slice off an antenna or another useful part with a cutting tool. Once the part is removed, the tender can attach it to a satlet before moving on to another dead satellite. Once it has all the parts it needs, it can launch the now fully operational satlet

into a higher orbit.

The entire process has been described as "delicate as surgery." Dropping an antenna or a solar panel in mid-orbit could have dangerous consequences. As David Barnhart, Phoenix's program manager put it, "For a person operating such robotics, the complexity is similar to trying to assemble, via remote control, multiple Legos at the same time while looking through a telescope."

Phoenix is currently looking for 10 old satellites it can use during test flights scheduled to begin in 2015. This is trickier than it sounds. There are an estimated 6,000 retired satellites and other objects floating around up there, and it can be tough to determine which organizations still own them. The program's goal is to reuse and recycle, not to snatch and grab.

But in the long run, those operators probably won't mind, as technology developed by the Phoenix Program may wind up saving them millions.

# FOR THE LONELY ASTRONAUT

What's the hardest part of being an astronaut, not counting the preciousness of oxygen, the threat of something going wrong at any moment, the possibility of being lost in space, or the body atrophying from extended periods in zero gravity? As Elton John once sang, "It's lonely out in space."

Japan's KIBO module on the International Space Station has a new resident: Robi, a 12-inch-tall, 2.2-pound humanoid robot, designed to keep astronaut Koicha Wakata from going stir-crazy. Other space programs have long used robots, but those were task-oriented robots. Robi, dressed in red boots and a white helmet, is purely social, outfitted with speech-recognition software, facial-recognition software (specifically, Wakata's face), and the ability to speak naturally. It can even tweet—both its own messages and Wakata's—back to Earth.

# SOCIAL ROBOTS

Facebook is so popular that even robots use it now. Researchers at the University of the United Arab Emirates' Interactive Robots and Media Lab, along with a group of scientists in Germany and Greece, teamed up in 2009 to see what would happen if they gave a Facebook page to a prototype, interactive robot named "Sarah."

Typically, people lose interest in an interactive robot once it has run out of pre-programmed questions and remarks. So the team gave Sarah an ever-growing pool of status updates and photos, and equipped it with the abilities to recognize faces in photos, post updates, and chat in real time. Whenever Sarah met a human for the first time, it was programmed to check their Facebook page and make comments about their most recent updates.

Sarah was also a bit gossipy and often posted details about various chats with humans on its page.

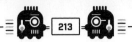

# SOCIAL (ARTIFICIAL) LIFE

We've all seen demonstrations of talking robots that state their names in mechanical-sounding voices and have the same basic personality as the GPS in your car. A Swedish robot, called "Furhat" because it inexplicably wears a fur trapper hat, has the ability to make direct eye contact and converse more like a regular human.

Most intriguingly, Furhat can take part in a chat with multiple participants: Sit down in front of the robot with a friend and it will ask both of you your names, inquire if and how you know each other, and shift his gaze back and forth between you like a normal (if too formal) person. Furhat is a bust mounted on a stand; he has no body or limbs, so despite his winning personality he isn't intended to do any physical work. Rather, his inventors suggest he could be stationed at assisted-living facilities to help keep confused elderly folks on track or be sold to lonely individuals to provide socialization and comfort.

# MOONRAKER 2.0

In 2009 NASA held the Regolith Excavation Challenge, calling for engineers to design a robot capable of digging up *regolith*, or moon dust, without requiring heavy machinery. To qualify, teams had to build robots that could excavate and unload at least 150 kg of regolith within a 30-minute period. The winner of the contest's $500,000 prize was the robotics team of the Worcester Polytechnic Institute, whose robot, Moonraker 2.0, beat out 22 teams by digging up a whopping 439 kg of regolith. Their invention was designed so well that it beat the second-place robot by nearly twice the payload! Moonraker 2.0 has become somewhat of a robotic celebrity, appearing at the Smithsonian National Air and Space Museum and even taking part at the groundbreaking ceremony for WPI's Sports and Recreation Center.

But is it as cool as James Bond foiling a moon-based poison-gas attack in 1979's *Moonraker*?

# YELLOW SUBMARINE

Ringo Starr was a prophet. Sure enough, a real-life, canary yellow U-boat lives beneath the waves in a sea of green. We can't all live on this yellow submarine, though. It's a giant robot.

Meet Sentry, an autonomous underwater vehicle designed to take bathymetric readings and explore hydrothermal fluxes (ocean depth and geothermal heat sources, respectively). Despite this nerdy, scientific background, Sentry is still quite the daring adventurer. It doesn't just dive four miles underwater—it dives four miles underwater into deep-sea volcanoes.

Since Sentry swims so far from its human handlers, it needs to be as smart as it is sturdy. Which is why Sentry is equipped with a space-age (sea-age?) artificial intelligence that can dynamically react to a sea of potential dangers, practically everything except a Sharkosaurus attack. Sentry's only real weakness is its bulky power source: 1,000 lithium batteries, just like the ones that power your laptop.

# GARDEN GNOME DRONE

Victoria, British Columbia, is known for its grand flower gardens, most particularly the Butchart Gardens. The biggest nuisance to gardens both big and small, in Victoria and out of Victoria, are scavenging animals such as deer and raccoons. What's also in Victoria: the University of Victoria's engineering department, where four students took military drone technology and shrank it down for use in keeping away unwanted garden guests.

The Garden Gnome Drone is based on a Parrot AR drone, about the size of a nightstand, consisting of three hoops connected by a pod of machinery and superfast propellers. The computer-vision navigation system onboard operates on an open-source Arduino microcontroller board. It's linked to infrared motion detectors placed around a yard—high for deer, low for raccoons and other small pests.

When an animal invades the garden, it trips a silent alarm, which sends the drone into action, dive-bombing the animal until it skedaddles.

# DO NOT CROSS THIS LINE

If armies were to give a robot the power to decide whether or not to use lethal force, they would want to make the decision black-and-white. South Korea maintains just such a black-and-white line with North Korea, and they now patrol the border with machine-gun robots.

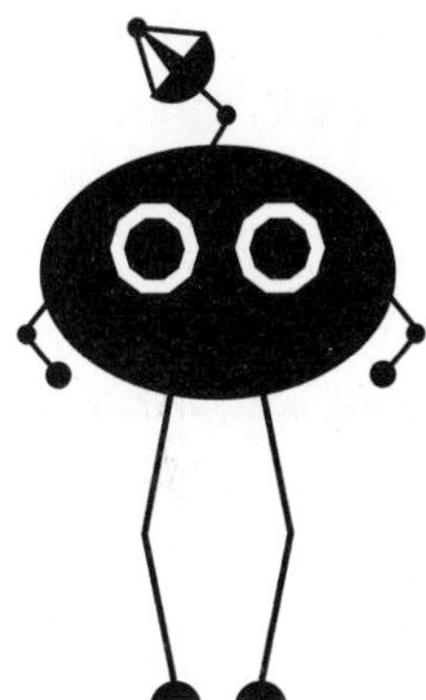

The robotic sentries are armed with guns capable of firing live or rubber bullets and, just for kicks, a rocket launcher. While they are designed to be operated remotely by a human being, the sentries can detect heat and motion, and can even prompt intruders for a password before mowing them down.

The technology is developed by Samsung, the tech giant whose Killing Machine department is apparently just down the hall from its TV and Blu-Ray player divisions.

# SNACKING ON PLASTIC

Remember those PSAs that implored you to snip the plastic holders of six-packs to protect marine life from accidentally getting stuck inside errant ones that drift out to sea? Well, there's a new plastic-based problem threatening ocean life: ever-growing gigantic islands of trash.

To combat this problem, designer Elie Ahovi has come up with an autonomous marine drone that patrols our oceans for trash. The drone looks like an orange trash can knocked over on its side, and it even sucks up garbage in the same place you would normally throw your junk away. To prevent fish and other marine life from getting sucked up, the drone sonically emits an annoying signal to deter live creatures. When the drone reaches its capacity, it will return to its mother ship where crew members can empty the drone of its contents.

At the moment, this drone is only a design, so keep snipping those plastic rings.

# "DON'T BE EVIL"

In the battle between software and hardware, Google has always been on the software side—creating algorithms, cataloging information, and providing cloud data storage. Software made Google rich, and now they're investing in hardware—specifically, robots.

In 2013 Google acquired *a dozen* of the world's top robotics firms. Chief among them: Boston Dynamics, the MIT-based firm specializing in military robots, like the cheetah-fast WildCat (see pg. 183). Why would Google be interested in building droids, drones, and bots? *They won't say.* Tech reporters suspect it has something to do with Google's commitment to self-driving cars.

Let's hope they're right. Google's corporate motto may be "Don't be evil," but the world's smartest computers teaming-up with the most-advanced robot soldiers doesn't sound completely on the level.

# ROBOT LAND

Since the Korean War, South Korea has surpassed its totalitarian neighbors to the north in almost every aspect: technologically, economically, politically, and culturally. But because of the Kim family's long-standing dictatorship, there's one facet of the isolated country that South Korea has yet to match: sheer craziness. So just like your annoying little brother, the south has decided to one-up their sibling to the north by creating a theme park made entirely of robots.

Originally announced in 2007 with a start date of 2009, Robot Land finally broke ground on construction in 2013. The $700 million, 8.1-million-square-foot theme park located in the city of Incheon is scheduled to be ready by 2016. The South Korean government hopes that Robot Land will become not only a tourist attraction but also an incubator for some of the region's most talented designers and engineers.

Here are some of the rides and attractions patrons can enjoy in a few years:

- **Robot Game Center/Convention Center:** A 2,000-seat exposition pavilion constructed

to showcase robot match-ups and to host the annual World Cyber Games tournament. (If you take your kids to Robot Land and they whine about not being able to play video games, this is where you drop them off.)

• **Robot Aquarium:** A giant tank featuring the park's cleverly named robotic-aquatic creations like "fish robot," "jellyfish robot," and "lobster robot."

• **Pavilion 3:** Did you ever go to an amusement park and think, "Boy, I wish I could see how a completely automated automobile-manufacturing plant works."? Then Pavilion 3 is the place for you.

• **Kidbot Village:** A section devoted to typical amusement-park rides, like roller coasters, Ferris wheels, and merry-go-rounds, all with a special theme: dragons! (Just kidding. It's robots.)

# GIVE UNTIL IT HURTS

When we think of "begging" and "robots," we usually imagine pitiful humans begging evil robots for their lives. But that may be about to change. These robots are the ones that beg, and they beg for spare change.

• GIM-E is a positronic panhandler built by artist Chris Eckert. Basically a rusty bucket with a "Gimme" sign, Eckert designed GIM-E to expose our reflexive "fear and anger" at human beggars.

• DON-8r ("donator") is a similar, albeit cuter, synthetic solicitor. It says "hello," "thank you," and motors around whenever you drop a coin in its slot. It didn't have much luck, earning $43 on its first three days on the job.

• Dona has done better, soliciting donations for Save the Children in New York's Union Square. Its key feature? Dona blinks helplessly, just like the homeless puppies from those ASPCA ads. Dona also frantically waves its arms to attract attention and ceremoniously bows as a thank-you.

# INHUMANNEQUINS

When someone mentions the lovely Kim Cattrall, the first place your mind goes is *Mannequin*, the 1987 romantic comedy in which she plays a sexy mannequin come to life. OK, maybe it doesn't come to your mind, but it almost certainly did for some advertising executive at United Arrows, a Japanese clothing store.

In an attempt to turn window shoppers into paying customers, United Arrows installed robot mannequins named MarionetteBots in the display windows of their Shibuya, Tokyo, store. The MarionetteBots are built with a motor and hooked up to Microsoft's Kinect, an Xbox 360 peripheral that allows families to play games by flailing their arms and legs in front of a motion-capture device. In this case, the Kinect is used to get families to buy clothes by shaking and dancing. While the MarionetteBots move in a slow, stiff manner, they do allow potential customers to see how the store's clothes would fit on them if they were slow, stiff robots.

# THE ROBOT ON THE WALL

What's arguably the most common robot in American homes? It's probably a dumb programmed mechanical novelty toy, and it's most likely made by a company called Gemmy Industries.

Operating out of Irving, Texas, Gemmy makes all manner of amusing programmed, battery-operated, talking robotic toys generally sold for "19.95!" and advertised on late-night TV, such as

• Big Mouth Billy Bass, a mounted large fish that comes to life to talk and sing;

• Buck the Animated Trophy, a mounted deer head that talks and sings.

They're also responsible for those full-size Halloween mannequins that terrify your children with their sudden robotic movements and realistic voices. The line includes horror-movie villains such as Freddy Krueger and Pinhead (from *Hellraiser*). Thanks a lot, Gemmy.

# JUNK IN THE TRUNK

If you were going to design and construct an agile and sophisticated robotic arm, what would you model it after? An arm? Don't be ridiculous. It stands to reason that human arms are somewhat imperfect, with all of those muscles, bones, and joints only bending a few directions. Perhaps that's why German tech company Festo took inspiration from an elephant's trunk in creating its bionic arm.

The Bionic Handling Assistant was introduced in 2010. An elephant can fluidly stretch and extend its trunk in any direction to grab an object. As can the BHA. At the end of the arm are four tiny grabbing claws. It's so precise that it can pick up an egg without breaking it.

Since the BHA is strong and delicate as well as agile, Festo says the robot's uses are many, from being an extra hand for handicapped patients to serving on industrial manufacturing lines, even picking fruit or milking (terrified) cows.

# KEEPON, KEEPIN' ON

Sometimes an expensive robot designed for research is just too darned cute not to market for mass consumption. Keepon, which looks like a combination of a marshmallow Peep and those squeezable stress-relief toys, was designed by Dr. Hideki Kozima as a tool to help children communicate. The tiny robot bobs his head and dances to music. And when you turn off the music, Keepon stops and looks around as if someone at a house party tripped over the speakers' cords. Because of its cute look, complete with yellow skin, cartoon eyes, and a button nose that also serves as a microphone, Keepon turned out to be a great tool for studying children with autism and other developmental disorders.

A toy company was contracted to mass-produce a less technologically-advanced home version of Keepon called My Keepon. The most difficult part: reducing the price from $30,000 to $40.

# MAKING THE CUT

Multi-Armed Unmanned Ground Vehicles (MA-UGVs) can disarm bombs, draw fire away from soldiers, and search for survivors at disaster sites. They can kick down doors, search backpacks for explosives, and cut wires...and hair.

A team at Intelligent Automation in Maryland wanted to see what would happen if they let a MA-UGV give somebody a buzz cut. Aided by three complex mechanical arms and a series of cameras, the robot's first customer was a courageous volunteer named Tim. The robot indeed shaved Tim's head, although Tim had the foresight to wear safety goggles—the MA-UGV wasn't very good at preventing falling hair from sliding down Tim's face.

Once it was all over, Tim was left looking like he had tried to cut his own hair. In the dark. While blindfolded.

# THE ROBOT HALL OF FAME

Baseball players have one. Rock stars have one. Even insurance agents have one (it's at the University of Alabama). So why not robots? Robotics' most magnificent marvels, both fictional and real, are celebrated at the Robot Hall of Fame in Pittsburgh on the campus of Carnegie Mellon, home to one of the country's leading robotics institutions.

Launched in 2003 by James Morris, the school's dean of computer science, the Hall aims to "honor robots that have served an actual or potentially useful function and demonstrated real skill, along with robots that entertain and those that have achieved worldwide fame in the context of fiction."

The hall has since inducted 29 robots from four categories: Education & Consumer; Research; Industrial & Service; and Entertainment—for fictional robots. The first inductees: HAL 9000, the evil robot from *2001: A Space Odyssey,* and the not-evil R2D2 from *Star Wars* Some of the other major inductees:

**Education & Consumer:** Sony's AIBO robotic pet dog; Lego's Mindstorms make-your-own robot kits; the Roomba (see pg. 142); and Nao (pg. 242).

**Entertainment:** Astro Boy (from the *Astro Boy* anime series); C-3PO (*Star Wars*); Robby the Robot (*Forbidden Planet*, 1956); Gort (*The Day the Earth Stood Still*, 1953); Maria (*Metropolis*, 1927); WALL-E (*WALL-E*, 2008); and the T-800 (*The Terminator*, 1984).

**Industrial & Service:** Unimate (see pg. 140); the da Vinci Surgical robot system; and SCARA, the four-axis robot arm developed in Japan.

**Research:** *Sojourner* (NASA's rover that explored Mars in 1997); Honda's ASIMO (pg. 89); Shakey, the first "thinking" robot (pg. 13); Carnegie Mellon's own Navlab 5, a self-driving car (pg. 133); and the fearsome BigDog (pg. 21).

# A SHOW OF HANDS

Perhaps creepier than a full-size mechanical man is a miniature robot that looks like a disembodied hand. Put your (human) hands together for the Sandia Hand. Developed by Sandia National Laboratories in New Mexico, the Sandia Hand has detachable fingers, and each finger can be replaced with a tool—some options include screwdrivers and flashlights, like some kind of Swiss Army Hand with electric power and a hint of autonomy.

Like most scary technological things, the Sandia Hand was designed for military use. In lab demonstrations, it has performed cute novelty acts, like inserting batteries into flashlights, and decidedly less cute functions, like dismantling explosives.

The Sandia Hand can be yours for $10,000, which is kind of a bargain, considering that today's top-of-the-line prosthetic hands cost $11,000 and don't do anything but sit there.

# A TAIL OF ROBOTS

Finally. Catlike robotic tails could make their way onto the backsides of the general human public by 2015.

Japanese company Neurowear has developed a fluffy tail that reacts to its wearer's heart rate and then acts out the appropriate emotion. "Tailly" wags excitedly from side to side with increased heart rate and slows to a relaxed pace when heart rate decreases. Creator Shota Ishiwatari believes that Tailly will not only add an element of excitement and playfulness to the lives of ordinary people, it will also bring couples closer together and help parents to better understand the true range of their children's emotions.

Tailly will be available in three colors (white, black, and tan) and is priced at an accessible $95. Neurowear also makes matching robotic ears to complete the look.

# ROCK 'EM, SOCK 'EM

In 1962 Burt Meyer of the design company Marvin Glass & Associates saw a mechanical game at a Chicago arcade: Two players each controlled a human figure, and the first player to hit the other's figure in the chin won. Glass liked the idea, so Meyer started making molds of human figures for a home version.

A few months later, boxing was suddenly very inappropriate for a toy. In a 1963 fight at Dodger Stadium, Sugar Ramos beat Davey Moore so badly that Moore fell into a coma and died. Glass told Meyer to stop working on the boxing game, but he had a better idea—change the human boxers to robots because "robots don't die." His other fix: the robots' heads would pop off when hit.

Glass sold the idea to Marx Toys, who began producing "Rock 'em Sock 'em Robots" in 1965. The game has been continually produced and sold ever since.

# DR. ROBOT, M.D.

Few things are more anxiety-provoking than being in a cold, sterile medical environment, at the mercy of some overworked healthcare provider who's looking to insert a tube or sharp object into your body. What if your nurse or doctor has shaky hands because he (or she) is hopped up on espressos or is distracted because he didn't have time to use the bathroom before your appointment?

To prevent the potentially bloody, painful consequences of such scenarios, a team of scientists based in Madrid is engineering a robot that can perform minor medical procedures. Surgical robots have existed in some form since 1984, but these machines are being developed for routine tasks, like administering injections, taking tissue samples, and inserting catheters.

Using a scanned image of the patient's anatomy, the robot is calibrated to ensure that the procedure is done smoothly and accurately, but that doesn't make a robot inserting a catheter any less unpalatable.

# BEST FRIENDS FOREVER

Remember how creepy Haley Joel Osment was as a little boy robot in *A.I. Artificial Intelligence*? Now imagine your kid going to school with him.

Students at Winchester Elementary School in Seneca Falls, New York, are learning to love their own robot classmate, a stand-in for Devon Carrow, a real boy living nearby. Carrow suffers from allergies so severe that leaving the house is a challenge. By age 7, he could still eat only infant formula, and contact with airborne peanut particles could send him to the ICU.

Since he couldn't attend school, Carrow acquired the VGo, a "telepresence robot." Not a humanoid robot, it's mostly a few metal rods on wheels with a TV monitor and a camera. It connects to the Internet, and Carrow's face appears on screen and his voice answers questions in class, which he sees via the camera's feed. A green light on the VGo indicates when Carrow is "raising his hand." With the help of the robot, Carrow can even appear on stage in class presentations.

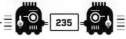

# A GOOD OLD-FASHIONED ROBOT WEDDING

In June 2007, in Daejeon, South Korea, a cone-shaped robot named "Tiro" became the first machine to officiate at a wedding. (The robot's designer, Seok Gyeongjae, was the bridegroom.)

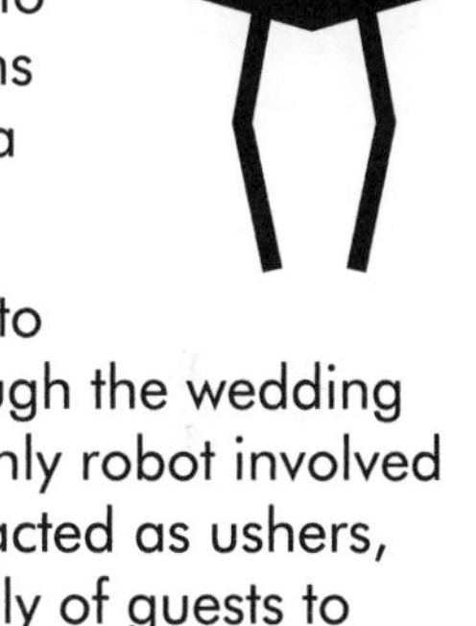

Tiro, which cost $215,000 to build, has two mechanical arms and a black glass "face" with a mouth of flashing red lights.

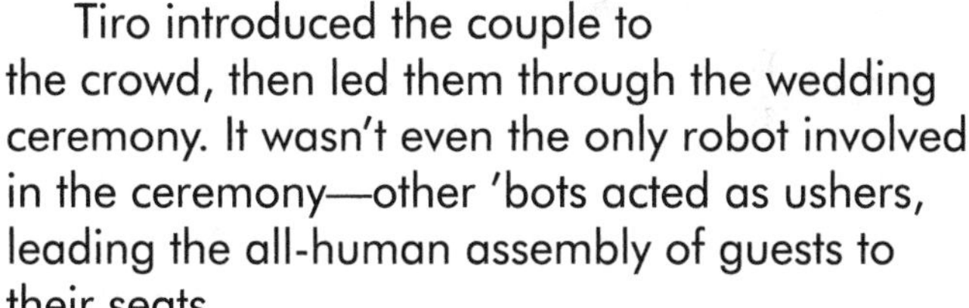

Tiro introduced the couple to the crowd, then led them through the wedding ceremony. It wasn't even the only robot involved in the ceremony—other 'bots acted as ushers, leading the all-human assembly of guests to their seats.

# BIONIC VISION

Most people associate bionic vision with either X-ray glasses that allow you to see through women's clothes, or the infrared crosshair screens used by the Terminator. Sadly, the Bionic Vision System isn't really like either of those things, but it is the type of stunning futuristic achievement that makes up for other junk our species has created, like the ShamWow.

Bionic Vision Australia is working on a "Bionic Vision System" to simulate sight for people with severe visual impairments. The system works via a microchip implanted in the retina (the sensory layer of the eye); the microchip receives data from a pair of special computerized glasses worn by the user.

To benefit from the system, patients must have either *retinitis pigmentosa* or age-related macular degeneration, because the optic nerve, visual cortex, and some retinal cells still function in people with these conditions. The Bionic Vision System doesn't completely restore sight, but rather creates a tableau of visual information out of phosphenes, or spots of light.

What does this really amount to for an otherwise visually impaired person? Bionic Vision Australia created an app to demonstrate what the user would see when using the system. The resulting images are black-and-white, pixillated versions of reality, sort of like looking at a photograph on a very low-res TV screen.

The level of detail that the user can see depends on the number of electrodes in the retinal implant; an earlier prototype has 98 electrodes, which results in enough resolution to avoid crashing into large objects when traversing a room. However, with 1024 electrodes, the "High-Acuity" model produces a sharp-enough image to allow users to read large-size text and recognize faces.

It's not quite as cool as Terminator vision, but it's definitely an amazing step forward for the visually impaired.

# DO THE ROBOT!

Engineers labor to make robots move more like humans, but for decades, humans have also been working to move more like robots... on the dance floor. Who needs a degree from MIT when you've got a cardboard square and a boom box?

Dancing The Robot involves sharp movements with abrupt starts and stops, imitating the gear-driven gesticulation characteristic of a science-fiction robot. The style grew out of other forms of street dancing, and elements of The Robot can be seen in 1960s soul and funk music performers, such as James Brown. One of its first recognized practitioners was the suitably nicknamed Charles "Robot" Washington, a *Soul Train* dancer in the early 1970s, who along with a few other performers came to be known as "The Robot Brothers."

But The Robot probably first gained prominence on the national stage when Michael Jackson performed it in a 1973 *Soul Train* performance with the Jackson 5. It's been a go-to for breakdancers ever since.

# IBOT WHEELCHAIR

Before its nationally televised unveiling, the Segway was hyped as a world-changing invention. But when the actual product turned out to be a gyroscope-enabled scooter, the Segway became an instant punchline, best known as the thing rich buffoon G.O.B. Bluth rode on *Arrested Development*. But Segway inventor Dean Kamen deserves a lot of credit for his invention that preceded the Segway: the iBot.

It looks like a standard, powered, four-wheel wheelchair. But unlike regular wheelchairs, each of the iBot's set of wheels can rotate around each other, allowing a user to climb stairs. The iBot could even stack its wheels on top of each other, which allowed its user to "stand" upright. Unfortunately, the iBot never caught on due to its five-figure price and prescription-only sales. Johnson & Johnson, who bought the product from Kamen, discontinued producing the iBot in 2009 and ended service for owners in 2013.

# RAVE RAFFE

The Burning Man festival in the Nevada desert is really an interactive art show, with thousands of attendees bringing sculpture, performance art, costume, or something else to share, all culminating in the ultimate art project: the destruction of a gigantic figure.

A light-show designer named Lindsay Lawlor used to attend Burning Man in a giraffe costume until a friend suggested that Lawlor use his electrical know-how to build a giraffe robot. So about 10 months before the 2006 iteration of Burning Man, Lawlor got to work on "Rave Raffe."

Lawlor sits in the metal exoskeleton lit up to resemble a giraffe, operating the hydraulically powered limbs. Lawlor can raise and lower the giraffe's long neck with a pneumatic pump. The giraffe weighs 1,700 pounds and operates on a 12-horsepower propane engine and three 450-amp batteries. It boasts 40 strobe lights, 400 LEDs...and cost Lawlor $15,000 to build, not counting what he could salvage from retired and unwanted industrial robots.

# LET'S SHAKE ON IT

Teleconferencing, using Skype for meetings, can feel a little impersonal, especially without the sacred businessman-bonding (and often legally binding) gesture of The Handshake. Of course, we have robots who can do that for us.

Engineers at Osaka University in Japan created a robotic hand that enables users to shake hands remotely. The hand is crafted out of silicone and sponge and sports a nifty film heater that is slightly above the average person's body temperature, so it's warm and gross, like a real businessman's hand.

Creators of the hand-bot hope that by adding a physical dimension to meetings that previously supported only visual and audio stimulus, individuals will feel at ease. Osaka's engineers hope to further improve their hand-bot by adding sensors that would mimic the user's strength of grip and speed of shake.

# NAO THAT'S A ROBOT!

For $8,000 you can get a used car, a first-class ticket from New York to Hong Kong, or 8,000 McDonald's McDoubles. But your best bet is Nao, a two-foot-tall humanoid robot. He's autonomous, adorable, and—for the first time ever—available to regular consumers.

Humanlike robots with the ability to learn new tasks have historically been built by and for academia and industry, and as such are extremely expensive. (Nao had similar beginnings—it was designed by a French company to play in an academic robot soccer league. Seriously.) Now anybody with a few thousand bucks and some programming knowhow can get their Nao to do almost anything they like.

Online you'll find awe-inspiring videos of Nao playing golf in a bathroom, Nao dancing "Gangnam Style," Nao petting a very uneasy cat, and more Nao dancing "Gangnam Style." It's a true testament to human ingenuity.

# ROBOT ALWAYS RELY ON KINDNESS OF STRANGERS

Artist Kacie Kinzer built a simple cardboard robot named Tweenbot, equipped with a smile and a flag adorned with the words "Help Me." As a social experiment, Kinzer programmed Tweenbot to be able to roll only straight forward, having to rely on assistance from strangers to successfully make it to a destination.

Hidden cameras were placed in New York's Washington Square Park to record Tweenbot's journey from one corner of the park to the other. Incredibly, 29 people stopped to help and direct Tweenbot, pulling it out from under park benches and even giving gentle, spoken advice, such as "Stay away from the road." It took just 42 minutes for Tweenbot to make its trip.

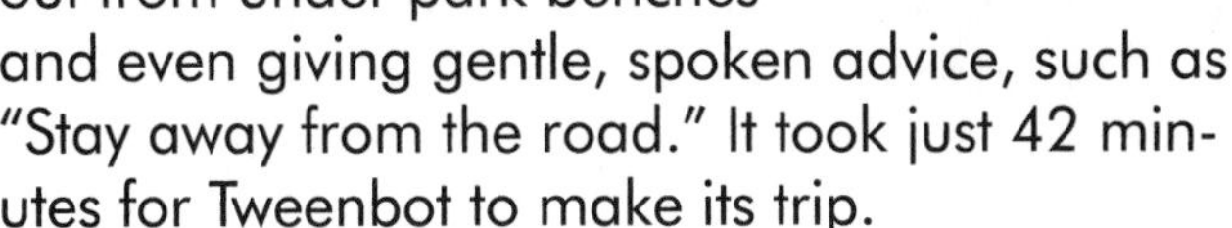

# BOWLING FOR BOTS

The United States Bowling Congress is not merely an organization to determine rules and host tournaments. It conducts high-minded bowling research, too. The Congress's Equipment Specifications and Certifications team is committed to improving the game by developing increasingly sleek and advanced equipment ranging from superfast ball-return machines to perfectly carved pins. The best tool at their disposal? E.A.R.L., a state-of-the-art robot that can bowl.

E.A.R.L. (short for **E**nhanced **A**utomated **R**obotic **L**auncher) debuted in October 2010. Unlike a human researcher, E.A.R.L. is capable of simulating any type of bowling style with consistency and accuracy. The robot, which sort of resembles one of those claw games found in arcades, can duplicate throws at speeds of anywhere from 10 to 24 mph, and at

revolution rates between 50 and 900 rpm. And he can do it all right- or left- "handed," and his arm never gets tired.

Following its debut, E.A.R.L. competed against pro bowler Chris Barnes. After just a few throws, the oil used to keep the average bowling lane slippery can change. E.A.R.L., who can only throw a ball from the exact same spot, couldn't adjust to the conditions by changing stances and positions like Barnes. Barnes won, 259 to 209.

# THE ROBOT THAT SAVED CHRISTMAS

Each year Neiman Marcus offers a luxurious and extravagant fantasy "His and Hers" Christmas package. It's a one-for-him and one-for-her of something fabulously impractical and expensive. In 1960 it was matching airplanes; in 1974, double hovercrafts. In 1981: robots.

The ComRo I was a domestic robot capable of opening doors and serving drinks with its hydraulic arm. Resembling a gas pump with lots of switches, it could also tidy up with its onboard vacuum hose. Other features of ComRo I that were exciting for 1981: a cordless telephone, a digital clock, and a black-and-white TV. Sold separately was ComRo I's pet and companion, Wires, a robot dog (if a dog looked like a bathroom scale with a mouse's head). Cost of ComRo I: $30,000 for two.

Neiman Marcus had contracted with the robot's developer, California roboticist Jerome Hamlin, who made them in his garage. Total number of ComRo I duos sold: three.

# YOU SIMPLY *MUST* GET A KLATU

*The Jetsons* made an imprint with its depiction of a future world in which men commuted in flying saucers, schools hovered above the clouds, and a robot named Rosie did all the housework. By way of Rosie, *The Jetsons* also influenced one of the biggest ever robot hoaxes.

In 1978, Quasar Electronics, primarily a TV manufacturer, announced a groundbreaking new product: Klatu, a five-foot-tall robot that could cook, clean, and walk the dog. There was just one problem: Klatu didn't quite exist yet.

But that didn't stop an executive at Quasar from announcing his company's life-changing creation or holding demonstrations to show off Klatu's abilities to skeptical journalists (a small person hid inside a Klatu suit). Despite causing a big stir among the public, Klatu was—obviously—never released.

# THE PIGEON PROBLEM

Garry O'Hagan, manager of Easter Road, a soccer stadium in Edinburgh, Scotland, was fed up with invading flocks of pigeons. They fouled the seats, annoyed the fans, and sometimes disrupted play on the field.

He wanted to find a humane way to get rid of the unwanted birds, so O'Hagan hired a pest-control expert who spent nine months developing Robop, an electronic robot peregrine falcon. But pigeons aren't easily fooled by most fake falcons, so this one was designed to flap its wings, move its head, and utter a realistic screech. It worked. Robop now stands guard over the stadium and scares the pigeons away.

# THE UNCANNY VALLEY

There is a place just over yonder where the robots are so lifelike, you might momentarily mistake them for human, and it will utterly creep you out: The Uncanny Valley.

As it turns out, we humans like our robots with human characteristics—think C-3PO, or Johnny 5 from *Short Circuit*—and that affinity grows the more humanlike they appear. But right at the point where the robot becomes so lifelike that we might not be able to tell the difference between it and a human, our love for the machine craters. Imagine that approval on a graph: growing steadily and then dropping like a stone. Robotics professor Masahiro Mori first researched and charted the phenomenon and coined the term "uncanny valley" for that drop-off point.

Mori postulates the phenomena follows a very basic human instinct: living things move; dead things do not. So it's no surprise he found only one thing that creeped humans out even more than lifelike robots: zombies.

# HATE THE ROBOTS!

You know what most of us would do with a robot if we had the chance? We'd pull the plug.

In 2007 robotics professor Christoph Bartneck tested human empathy for artificial intelligence. People were placed in a room with a computer and a robot cat; they played a game where in some cases, the robot was helpful, and in others, the robot was not. The robots also demonstrated varying levels of social skill; some were kind, others were rude. At the end of the game, the test subjects were told to turn off the robot, which would eliminate all of its personality and memories. Meanwhile, the robot would essentially beg for its life, pleading, "You're not really going to switch me off, are you?"

In every case, the human managed to switch off the robot, although in some cases, it took up to 35 seconds for the human to complete the task. A few test subjects began debating with the robot or apologizing for being required to end the robot's life.

# PITY THE ROBOTS!

These poor defenseless robots! All they want to do is serve humanity, and what do they get for it? Abused, mistreated, and deeply mistrusted. And for that, we pity them.

Astrid Rosenthal-von der Putten is a researcher in Germany who noted passionate feelings for robots when she saw the emotional comments on an online video of a robot dinosaur being tortured. To learn more, she set up a simple study: 40 people watched videos of a person cuddling and then abusing a baby dinosaur robot. Her team monitored physiological responses of the subjects to the video, that is, they measured how much they sweat. (Science!)

Results: Subjects sweat more, and thus felt bad, when they watched the robot getting hurt. A second study paired the dinosaur videos with similar videos depicting a human woman being shown affection or anger. The subjects viewing the videos responded the same whether they were watching a robot or a human.

# RANDOM ROBOT FACTS

• Nine out of 10 robots that exist today work in factories—more than half make automobiles.

• In 1942 science-fiction writer Isaac Asimov proposed three "laws of robotics" to ensure the safety of humankind. The first law: "A robot may not injure a human being, or, through inaction, allow a human being to come to harm." In 2006 Japan made Asimov's law an actual law. The country that gave us Godzilla is developing robot nurses (for elder care), but they fear robot rebellion. So all robots must now have sensors to prevent them from running into people, be made of soft materials, and include emergency shut-off buttons.

• The U.S. military uses Roomba-like robots to scout out enemy hideouts. It's been reported, however, that rebels in Afghanistan figured out how to outwit the robots—they stick a ladder under them and flip them over.

• Only 38 percent of Internet traffic is human. The rest is comprised of web-trolling bots.

• *Automatonophobia* is the fear of robots.

• While filming *The Passion of the Christ*, actor Jim Caviezel (playing Jesus) risked hypothermia enduring 15-hour days hanging on a cross wearing only a loincloth. So filmmakers constructed a body double: a $220,000 robot that looked like Caviezel and was able to move its head and limbs convincingly.

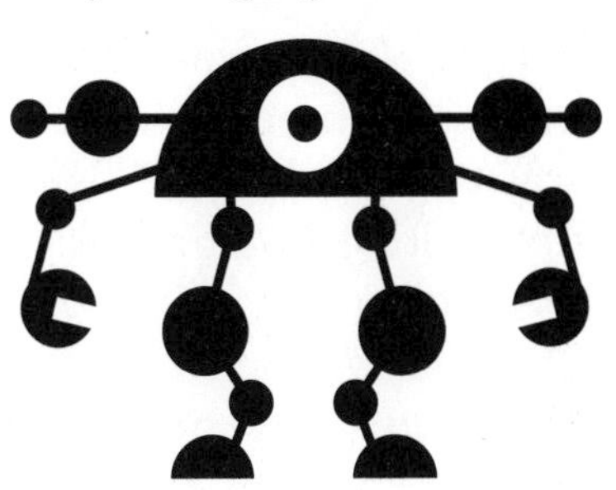

• The Raëlians are a religious group that believe life on Earth was created via genetic engineering by an advanced alien race. The religion's "prophet" is a former sports journalist named Claude Vorilhon, who now calls himself "Raël." He claims one of these aliens, named Yahweh, visited him and told him the truth. In 1975, he says, Yahweh took Raël to an interstellar spa, then deposited him in his apartment, where several beautiful lady robots made love to him.

# OMINOUS BOT THOUGHTS

"Who is the living food for the machines in Metropolis?"

**—False Maria, *Metropolis***

"I wish I had more time to discuss this, but I must explode in seventy-five seconds."

**—Bomb #20, *Dark Star***

"Four…three…two…one…I am now authorized to use physical force!"

**—ED-209, *RoboCop***

"Take him for a drive. And bring me back his exact weight in paper clips."

**—Phineas T. Ratchet, *Robots***

"All those moments will be lost in time…like tears in rain…Time to die."

**—Roy Batty, *Blade Runner***

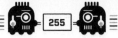

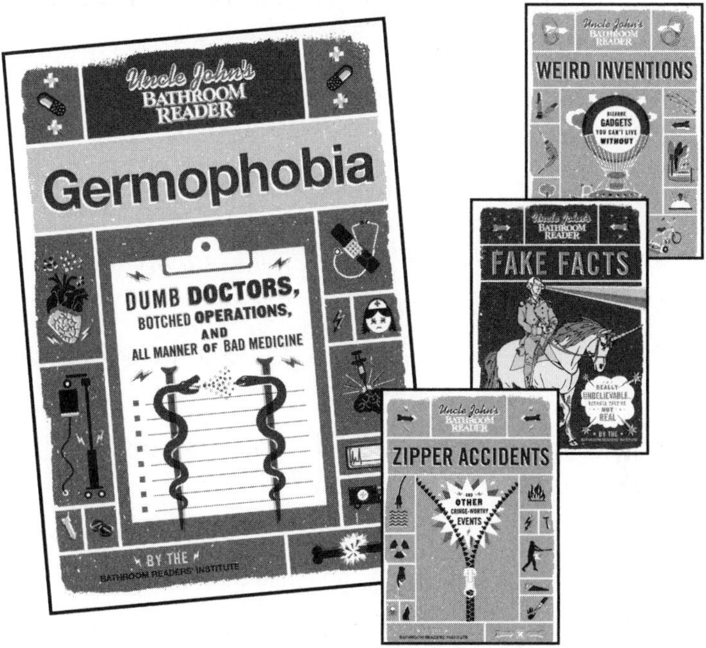

# THE LAST PAGE

**FELLOW BATHROOM READERS:**

The fight for good bathroom reading should never be taken loosely—we must do our duty and sit firmly for what we believe in, even while the rest of the world is taking potshots at us.

We'll be brief. Now that we've proven we're not simply a flush-in-the-pan, we invite you to take the plunge:

Sit Down and Be Counted! Log on to www.bathroomreader.com and earn a permanent spot on the BRI honor roll!

---

If you like reading our books...
VISIT THE BRI'S WEBSITE!
*www.bathroomreader.com*

- Receive our irregular newsletters via e-mail
- Order additional *Bathroom Readers*
- Face us on Facebook
- Tweet us on Twitter
- Blog us on our blog

Go with the Flow...

---

Well, we're out of space, and when you've gotta go, you've gotta go. Tanks for all your support. Hope to hear from you soon.

Meanwhile, remember...

**KEEP ON FLUSHIN'!**